Praise for *Plan of Life*

"From routine tasks to complex projects and special events, if we are going to be successful, we need to have a plan. Father Landry provides us a practical, accessible, and very helpful means of developing a plan for living our faith and growing in holiness. At a time when so many voices are competing for our attention, and some calling us in the wrong direction, this book guides us through the steps of strengthening our spiritual life and our participation in the life of the Church. I highly recommend it for anyone who has recognized the need for a better spiritual focus in their daily life but doesn't know where or how to begin. With great generosity, humility, and devotion to the Lord and our Blessed Mother, Father Landry shows us the way forward."

— Séan Cardinal O'Malley, OFM, Cap.,
Archbishop of Boston

"A successful spiritual life needs the same discipline that a successful diet or physical training requires. Father Landry's very helpful book prompts us to develop such a regimen for growth in holiness. It's hardly a 'self-help' book, but a 'soul-help' one, reminding us on each page that the *real help* comes only from the Lord."

— Timothy Michael Cardinal Dolan,
Archbishop of New York

"Many of us try to squeeze God into our crowded life rather than seek to center our life around God. Father Landry not only shows us the path to unite our life to God but also accompanies us step by step in that transformation. This book will change you and may be just what you need to find the life you've always wanted and that God has wanted for you."

— Archbishop Bernardito C. Auza, Apostolic Nuncio,
Permanent Observer of the Holy See to the United Nations

"The ultimate goal of the life of every Christian is union with the Blessed Trinity and eventually to be a saint. As Father Landry says, 'Every major goal in life requires a plan.' We plan our days, weeks, months, and years. We plan our appointments, activities, commitments, work, and business. How about planning our spiritual life? Father Landry shows in this book how to plan our spiritual journey so that we don't get lost on the way."

— Most Reverend Edgar da Cunha, Bishop of Fall River

"Father Roger Landry is one of the leaders of the New Evangelization in the United States. His advice on how to be the missionary disciples we were all baptized to be is always thoughtful, engaging, and welcome."

— George Weigel, Distinguished Senior Fellow
and William E. Simon Chair at the Catholic Studies,
Ethics and Public Policy Center; author of *Witness to Hope*

"Jesus calls us to friendship with him. How do we take up this wonderful invitation? Father Landry distills the Church's wisdom and provides what we all need—good counsel that's at once practical and spiritual. This is the perfect book for all Christians who want to drink more deeply from the spring of living water that wells up to eternal life.

— R. R. Reno, editor of *First Things*

"'No one plans to fail, but many fail to plan.' Father Roger Landry has written an enormously helpful book for those planning to get to heaven. By explaining in clear and simple language the time-tested method of a 'Plan of Life,' Father Landry's book will encourage and inspire even the most lukewarm soul to become a better Christian. A must-have book for your spiritual reading library."

— Reverend Francis J. "Rocky" Hoffman, executive director of Relevant Radio

"Father Landry was born to be a coach of the spiritual life. And this is the most accessible manual you could pick up for being seriously, joyfully Catholic now, in the busy-ness of your life. Your imitation of Christ will only grow if you follow this holy priest's advice."

— Kathryn Jean Lopez, Senior Fellow of the National Review Institute; editor-at-large of *National Review;* nationally syndicated columnist

"Lots of people want to improve their spiritual lives and some make repeated efforts to do so. But many fail from not having personal guidance or a workable plan, something we would seek in any other part of life. Father Roger Landry's approach is not only clear and easy to follow, it's lively and spiritually enlightening on every page. One can't help but benefit from the wisdom and practical advice he offers. This is a book to read, and to keep handy to reread often."

— Robert Royal, Faith & Reason Institute

"To have a plan for daily living is posited on the premise that there is a purpose for life. This may seem obvious, but in our culture there are sad rumors that there is no reason for living beyond managing to exist. Since the Spirit gives life, spiritual practices are at the heart of living, and Father Landry suggests in clear and amiable ways, rather like Francis de Sales and Alphonsus Liguori, what this means."

— Father George William Rutler, author; pastor of St. Michael Parish, New York City

"The late Father Bob Bedard, founder of Canada's Companions of the Cross, told thousands of people the secret to a good spiritual life: 'The decision not to go to bed on time is a decision not to pray the next morning.' Rather simple. And true. Father Landry, in this most practical of books, takes you from that bedtime moment, to waking the next morning, to bedtime again and shows how—with work and study and family—you can consecrate that time to God. If you don't have a 'plan of life' you won't grow in friendship with God. You don't *have* to use this book, but why make it more difficult to begin without it?"

— Father Raymond de Souza, editor in chief
of *Convivium* magazine

"Father Landry has given us an easy-to-read guide on living a daily Catholic spiritual program that is challenging and rewarding, but not impossibly burdensome. He presents and explains various norms of piety that nourish us in our struggle to grow closer to God. This book informs, inspires, and encourages: you can grow in love for God by taking time to pray at different points throughout the day."

— Father Gerald E. Murray, pastor of Holy Family Church,
New York; member of EWTN's "Papal Posse"

"At a time when many Christians feel buffeted by the rising tide of secularism, Father Roger Landry's book is the ideal guide to higher and better ground. *Plan of Life* is nothing less than a beautiful answer to the prayer, 'Show me and my family how to live.' It's the perfect gift for Confirmation, graduation, birthdays, and every other milestone that's celebrated in this world while pointing to the next."

— Mary Eberstadt, author of *How the West Really
Lost God* and *Adam and Eve after the Pill*

"I have twice been on pilgrimages to Rome with Father Landry and experienced, with other journalists, his opening up of the great treasures of faith there. So it is no surprise to see him offer here a brilliant little treasure chest of spiritual practices. Most people have a desire to grow closer to God but don't know how. Herein lies a map.

— Peggy Noonan, Pulitzer Prize-winning columnist,
Wall Street Journal

"Father Landry was instrumental in helping me embrace the Catholic faith. He has a way of explaining the faith with clarity, passion, and beauty. Reading this book has strengthened my faith and will help strengthen yours!"

— Kirsten Powers, CNN political commentator,
USA Today columnist, author of *The Silencing*

"We live in an age of spiritual junk food that brings momentary comfort, but little nutrition. This book is an eighteen-course meal of nourishment—bite-size portions that will bolster your spiritual health while provoking longings for the heavenly banquet. As a member of my 'Conclave Crew' during the election of Pope Francis, Father Landry made the most arcane details of Church history and doctrine accessible to everyone. His usual brilliance and heartfelt concern for souls is evident on every page of this much-needed book."

— Raymond Arroyo, *New York Times* best-selling author,
lead anchor of EWTN's *The World Over Live*

"We like to plan out every aspect of our celebrations, our travel, and even our errand running, yet so often we leave our spiritual lives up to chance and then wonder why we're not getting anywhere. Here, like a good coach, Father Landry reveals the 'game-plan' by which we can truly deepen our prayer lives, grow in our outreach, and pursue holiness. *Plan of Life* is a practical and inspiring exhortation to take up the tools, practices, and sacraments of the Church and use them to build a spiritual life that is ingrained, structured, and oriented toward heaven."

— Elizabeth Scalia, author of *Strange Gods: Unmasking the Idols in Everyday Life*

Plan of Life

Plan of Life

HABITS TO HELP YOU GROW CLOSER TO GOD

By Roger J. Landry

Foreword by Matthew Kelly

Pauline
BOOKS & MEDIA

Library of Congress Cataloging-in-Publication Data

Names: Landry, Roger J., author.

Title: Plan of life : habits to help you grow closer to God / Fr. Roger J. Landry.

Description: Boston, MA : Pauline Books & Media, 2018.

Identifiers: LCCN 2017021184| ISBN 9780819860439 (pbk.) | ISBN 0819860433 (pbk.)

Subjects: LCSH: Spiritual life--Catholic Church. | Christian life--Catholic authors.

Classification: LCC BX2350.3 .L35 2018 | DDC 248.4/82--dc23

LC record available at https://lccn.loc.gov/2017021184

Published by Pauline Books & Media, 50 Saint Pauls Avenue, Boston, MA 02130-3491

Printed in the U.S.A.

www.pauline.org

Pauline Books & Media is the publishing house of the Daughters of St. Paul, an international congregation of women religious serving the Church with the communications media.

2 3 4 5 6 7 8 9   22 21 20 19 18

To the members of the domestic church
where I first learned to know, love, and serve
God and others.

Contents

BEYOND THE BASICS

Foreword

"Those who fail to plan can plan to fail." This was Benjamin Franklin's counsel to a group of businessmen setting out on a new venture. We plan for so many things in life, but astoundingly very few people have a plan for the most important aspect of life—the spiritual one. And the uncomfortable truth, the often unspoken truth, is that without a plan to grow spiritually, we will fail in many areas of our lives and almost certainly fail to live the rich and fruitful life God created us to live.

In some ways it is easier than ever before to establish a Plan of Life that helps us grow spiritually. This book is a perfect example of that. One hundred years ago, monthly meetings with a great spiritual director for years would have been necessary to learn what you will discover between the covers of this book.

In other ways, however, it is harder than ever to establish a plan of life. The pace of our lives and all we cram into them, the noise of our lives and all the many voices we choose to pay attention to, all prevent us from sinking the roots of regular spiritual habits deep into our daily lives.

These deep roots are essential. They are essential to encounter and befriend the living God; they are essential to discover the-best-version-of-ourselves; they are essential to live with clarity in a world of confusion; they are essential to find peace in a culture of chaos; and they are essential to experience the joy of being alive and blessed and loved. Deep roots are simply essential for these and so many other reasons. But there is one reason in particular I would like to explore with you.

When a storm blows through town, there are always trees that get blown over and branches that are broken. Why do some trees blow over and others don't? Roots. Deep roots. Strong roots. A tree with deep, strong roots can weather any storm.

And life is full of storms. The question is not, will there be a storm? The question is, when is the next storm getting here? And when the storm arrives, it's too late to think about sinking roots. At that point, you either have them or you don't.

Father Roger Landry is one of the great voices of clarity in our times of confusion. He is a friend to your soul. In these pages he will be your spiritual guide. Chapter by chapter, he presents the great spiritual practices that will help you to build a Plan of Life.

This book is like the man. It will inspire you to want to live a holy life. Every time I am with Father Landry, I walk about inspired, filled with hope, and hungry to be a better person and live a better life. These pages are dripping with that kind of hope and inspiration.

Over these twenty-five years that I have been speaking and writing, I have become absolutely convinced that there is one primary, immutable truth when it comes to living as a Christian in the world. It is this: the Christian life is simply not sustainable without daily prayer. This is the first root to sink deep into our lives. If you don't already have a firmly established habit of daily prayer, this book will help you to establish one. It will become one of the great joys of your life.

But reading these pages, I am led to conclude: it is impossible to excel in the Christian life without a Plan of Life. And that is what we are called to: excellence. We think about achieving excellence in so many areas of our lives, but when was the last time you reflected seriously on achieving excellence in the spiritual life?

Let this book be the beginning. Let it be your beginning. People don't live holy lives accidentally. It happens on purpose. It will never be convenient to build a Plan of Life like Father Landry describes in this book. But the day you decide to set out along that path is a day you will remember forever. I hope today is that day for you.

MATTHEW KELLY
Founder of Dynamic Catholic

Preface

So You Want to Grow Closer to God?

Imagine yourself on your deathbed. Your family and friends surround you. You are full of peace and joy because you are confident that you have lived a good life. You have gone through much of your life with faith, purpose, peace, and charity. You have come to know and love Jesus through Scripture and the Eucharist. You have gradually become more and more like Jesus by growing in virtue and union with him. And now you are getting ready to meet and embrace him whom you have strived to serve and to love. You hear him say to you, in his mercy, the words he told us he longs to say to everyone, "Well done, my good and faithful servant. . . . Come, share your Master's joy" (Mt 25:21, *NABRE*).

Do you think your last moments will be like this? Do you want them to be?

There is no better time than now to start living in a way that will help your last moments be those of peace rather than regrets. No one lays on his deathbed wishing that he had spent more time watching TV, surfing the Internet, or working.

As a priest who has assisted hundreds of people on their death-beds, I can tell you that many spend their last moments wishing that they had done the more important things in life, such as being with their families.

But the most important activity of all is prioritizing time with the One with whom we hope to spend eternity. As important as our relationships are with a spouse, parents, children, and friends, the most important relationship of all is with our Creator and Redeemer. Without him, after all, no other relationship would be possible.

It is our relationship with God that matters most.

Every major goal in life requires a plan. Succeeding in the test of life and passing with God from death to eternity is the most important end of our human existence. This book attempts to lay out a plan for the ultimate goal a person can ever have in life: loving union with God.

Are you ready to work on your relationship with God? To put God first? To live as his "good and faithful servant"?

If so, let's get started.

How to Use This Book

When you put a Plan of Life into practice, it is good to remember that no one can do everything at once. This book is full of practices that you can choose to incorporate gradually into your life. It's possible that you might feel overwhelmed as you make your way through the book, especially if the majority of the practices are new to you. But I would encourage you, in the words of Jesus and Saint John Paul II, "Be not afraid!" This is not a book of demands. Rather, it is a treasure chest of practices that will help you respond to God's help to become holier, happier, and grow closer to him every day.

I urge you to read through this book prayerfully and allow the chapters to serve as conversation starters for a dialogue with God about your life. He knows where you are spiritually as well as all your commitments, struggles, and joys. Let God help you to see which practices can be integrated right away to grow in greater union with him and which can wait. Don't hesitate to ask him for help when and how you need it. It might be good to stop for at least a brief one-on-one with God at the end of every chapter.

In the first part of the book, "The Basics," we will focus on the fundamentals for growth in the spiritual life. Then you will have a chance to pause and take an inventory. At that point you can reflect on what you're already doing well, what you're doing but could do better, and which practices you have perhaps not even considered as being part of your spiritual life. It will be an opportunity to water some of the seeds that God may have planted so that they might grow and bear fruit.

In the second part of the book, "Beyond the Basics," we'll focus on those habits that might assist you to grow even more. And at the end of the book, a worksheet and the resources in the appendices will help you formulate and begin to keep a Plan of Life.

You've certainly taken a step in the right direction by picking up this book. I hope that you will find what I have discovered personally and in my pastoral work with many others at all stages in their journey: that formulating and following a solid spiritual Plan of Life is one of the most important and life-enhancing decisions any of us can make!

Introduction

Jumpstart Your Spiritual Life

"No disciple is superior to the teacher; but when fully trained, every disciple will be like his teacher." (Lk 6:40, *NABRE*)

To become like Jesus, to follow him, to imitate him, and to love God and others with our whole heart and mind is the deepest reason for our existence. At a sacramental level, we are conformed to Christ in Baptism, but most of us, at a moral level, have a long way to go to become more like Jesus. The whole mission of the Church is to help people to become more like Jesus, to become saints. Over the centuries, the Church has needed to sledgehammer the heresy that holiness is the calling of only a few. Rather, the call to holiness comes from our Baptism and the ways to sanctity are many.

God the Father's ultimate desire, shown in the great lengths to which he went in Jesus' suffering, death, and Resurrection, is that all of us will one day share eternal life with him. For that desire to be realized, however, our cooperation is required. Saint Augustine once wrote that though God created us without our consent, he won't save us without our consent. To become a saint and eventually enter heaven, we must will it. Jesus spoke powerfully about that willing in the Gospel. He said that we need to "strive to enter through the narrow door" that leads to heaven (Lk 13:24). Which road we're on, which road we'll seek to be on, and whether we're heading toward or away from holiness, happiness, and heaven, involves the most consequential decisions of our life.

Saint John of the Cross wrote that we were born "for no other reason than to be a saint." French intellectual Léon Bloy once stated that life's only great tragedy is *not* to become holy—not just because of the potential eternal consequences, but because one would go through life without establishing the friendship with God that makes life most meaningful.

Willing holiness, however, is not enough. As Peter realized, much to his dismay on Holy Thursday night, "The spirit indeed is willing, but the flesh is weak" (Mt 26:41). We need something that can strengthen our frail flesh to align itself with our willing spirit. The reality is that becoming like Jesus is the work of a lifetime. We need what Saint John Paul II called a "genuine training in holiness, adapted to people's needs." We need a Plan of Life, a "game plan" for our spiritual life.

In almost every sphere of life, a person who takes something seriously comes up with a plan. Success depends on a solid plan and perseverance. Championship sports teams, flourishing businesses, triumphant political campaigns, and successful people all teach us a powerful lesson: those who get results are generally the ones with better strategies. There's got to be a plan. It's got to be a good plan. And you have to stick to that plan.

The same is true of the spiritual life. There's no reason why we shouldn't take our spiritual plan just as seriously as sports teams that train and strategize, and dieters who count calories and plan what they eat. The spiritual life is too important to wing. So much of our happiness, in this world and in the next, depends on whether we have a Plan of Life, whether it's adequate to form us in holiness, and whether we make and keep the commitment to follow our plan.

In the early Church, Saint Paul specialized in providing training in the Christian life. His letters are full of advice from an expert coach in the spiritual life. Paul urged parents to raise their children "in the discipline and instruction of the Lord," and he provided the same training for his spiritual children (Eph 6:4). "I am again in the pain of childbirth," he wrote to the Galatians, comparing himself to a mother, "until Christ is formed in you" (Gal 4:19).

Paul urged the young Saint Timothy, "Train yourself in godliness, for, while physical training is of some value, godliness is valuable in every way, holding promise for both the present life and the life to come" (1 Tim 4:7–8). Paul followed his own advice, telling the Corinthians, "I do not run aimlessly, nor do I box as though beating the air; but I punish my body and enslave it, so that after proclaiming to others I myself should not be disqualified" (1 Cor 9:26–27).

Paul's spiritual training involved years of prayer and study in the Arabian Desert. He suffered a "thorn . . . in the flesh," and battled "against the spiritual forces of evil" (2 Cor 12:7; Eph 6:12). Paul endured multiple assassination attempts, shipwrecks, scourging, stoning, betrayals, imprisonments, sleepless nights, hunger and thirst, cold and exposure, opposition, and so much more.

But through it all, Paul was able to "have the mind of Christ," adopt Christ's attitude, and vest himself with God's armor of truth and holiness (see 1 Cor 2:16). So thorough was his training that he was eventually able to tell the Galatians, "It is no longer I who live, but it is Christ who lives in me" (Gal 2:20).

Christian training can take on many different forms. (Hopefully yours will not involve years in the Arabian Desert!) But Jesus is constantly trying to do for us what he did for Saint Paul: give us, through the Church, a full training, so that we may become more and more like him and he can truly and increasingly live in us.

At this point, you may be asking yourself, "How can I train to become more like Christ?"

The Church has a treasure trove of saint-making tips and spiritual practices. From the example of Christ in Scripture, to the model of the early Christian martyrs, to the lives of canonized men and women from all walks of life, we have learned many ways to become more like Christ.

Saint John Paul II summed up the Church's wisdom regarding attaining union with God by naming six pillars of "training in holiness": grace, prayer, Sunday Mass, Confession, listening to the word of God, and proclaiming that word.

Making sure each of these pillars is present in our lives, however, does not guarantee sanctity. We need not just to do them, but also to get the most out of them and integrate them into our daily lives. We must prayerfully work with God to develop a "curriculum" of spiritual formation—something similar to the "rules" found in consecrated communities—designed to help those who follow them grow in holiness day by day.

That program of spiritual formation is generally called a Plan of Life, which is a game plan of spiritual exercises to help people learn how to fight the good fight, to run the race of life so as to win, and to keep the faith by growing in faith and sharing it (see 2 Tim 4:7; 1 Cor 9:14). It's a series of practices given to us by the saints and spiritual directors to help people to translate their desire to grow closer to God from a vague aspiration into a reality.

Developing a Plan of Life may sound frightening, but remember that growth in the spiritual life is an exciting invitation, not a chore. And any good plan involves making small steps in the right direction. A plan for holiness of life is no different.

THE
BASICS

CHAPTER 1

The Holy Spirit

A Sanctifying Fire

The purpose of a Plan of Life is to help us grow in holiness. But it's essential to focus primarily on the work of sanctification that God is trying to accomplish in us rather than on our own efforts. Saint Paul tells us that the Holy Spirit carries out the work of sanctification (see Rom 15:16). The Holy Spirit worked a miraculous metamorphosis in the lives of the first members of the Church on Pentecost, changing them from apostates to apostles, from chickens to shepherds. When we consider how the Holy Spirit worked in the lives of the first members of his Church, it is fitting also to ponder whether the Holy Spirit is truly the guide of our day-to-day life as well.

During the Last Supper, Jesus described how important the Holy Spirit is when he said, "I tell you the truth: it is to your advantage that I go away, for if I do not go away, the Advocate will not come to you; but if I go, I will send him to you" (Jn 16:7). Jesus was saying that if we had to choose between him and the Holy Spirit, we should choose the latter: that's how important the Holy Spirit is! Obviously, the great joy is that we don't have to choose, because God the Father, Son, and Holy Spirit is a Trinitarian unity. But it's still key to understand that if we take Jesus seriously, if we take God the Father seriously, we need to take the Holy Spirit just as seriously.

The unfortunate reality, however, is that the Holy Spirit remains "the great unknown" in so many people's lives. When Saint Paul came to Ephesus and met some disciples, he asked, "Did you receive the Holy Spirit when you became believers?" They responded, "No, we have not even heard that there is a Holy Spirit" (Acts 19:2).

Pope Benedict XVI once said, "The Holy Spirit has been in some ways the neglected person of the Blessed Trinity." Benedict confessed that it was only as a young priest that he began to recognize the importance of the Holy Spirit and came to know him more intimately. Benedict stressed that the Holy Spirit is the highest gift of God to humanity. If we wish to understand the faith, if we wish to live it, if we wish to pass it on, we must allow the Holy Spirit to become the guide of our souls, even if, like the young future pope Joseph Ratzinger, we begin later in life. For us, the "great unknown" must become the "great known," our Teacher, Leader, Consoler, and Advocate. We must come to consider him, as did Pope Benedict XVI, "the highest gift of God to mankind."

As Catholics, how can we grow in our relationship with the Holy Spirit so that he can carry out his work of sanctification in us? The best way is to allow him into every area of our life, since holiness is about living fully in communion with God.

To illustrate the difference the Holy Spirit can make if we let him, we can focus on a few areas.

The first area where the Holy Spirit helps us is in our prayer. Saint Paul tells us, "The Spirit helps us in our weakness; for we do not know how to pray as we ought, but that very Spirit intercedes

with sighs too deep for words" (Rom 8:26). The Holy Spirit
teaches us how to pray. He does this not principally by putting
words in our minds and mouths, but *by changing who we are* as we
pray. The Holy Spirit helps us to be conscious of our reality as
beloved sons and daughters of God the Father, able to cry out confidently "Abba!" or "Father!" or "Daddy!" (Gal 4:6).

Do we allow the Holy Spirit to guide our prayer? One simple
way to do this, if you don't already, is to start any type of prayer,
including preparation for Mass, with a prayer to the Holy Spirit.

The second area the Holy Spirit helps with is in our daily living,
which is meant to be a life "according to the Spirit," seeking the
things of the Spirit and putting to death the things of the flesh (Rom
8:5). Life according to the Spirit is authentic Christian spirituality;
someone who lives indulgently is not, as some claim, genuinely spiritual, but carnal. To be spiritual means to follow the Spirit's guidance
throughout the day, seeking to live by his wisdom, knowledge,
understanding, prudence, courage, reverence, and awe (see Is 11:2).
It means consciously allowing the Holy Spirit to guide us and influ-
ence the choices we make. Living by the Spirit means recognizing
that each of us has been given a "manifestation of the Spirit" for the
common good and striving to use those gifts for God and others (1
Cor 12:7). It also means allowing and accepting that the Holy Spirit
will occasionally prevent our doing even good things to guide us in
other directions (see Acts 16:6–7).

Do we allow the Holy Spirit to guide the nitty-gritty details of
our daily life? One good practice is to pause at the beginning of an
activity and simply pray, "Come, Holy Spirit!" Another is to ask
for his light whenever we have to make an important decision. A
third is to stop and ask in which direction the Holy Spirit, whom
Jesus says is like the wind that "blows where it chooses," is trying to
move me now (Jn 3:8).

The third way the Holy Spirit helps us is in our sharing our faith. The Holy Spirit came upon the first members of the Church as tongues of fire so that they could proclaim the Gospel with ardent love (see Acts 2:3). The Holy Spirit helps us to be witnesses of the faith. Jesus promised that the Holy Spirit would teach us all things, lead us to all truth, give us the words we need under trial, and remind us of everything Jesus had taught, precisely so that we could give this witness (see Jn 14:26; Mk 13:11). Our sanctification involves our cooperation in the Spirit's work to complete Jesus' mission of the salvation of the world.

Do our lives give evidence of tongues of fire and burning hearts? One way we can determine the answer is to ask whether we honestly are yearning to share the gift of our faith with others. We also can consider whether we are asking the Holy Spirit to inspire our words and actions so that we may give authentic witness to the light of God's truth and the warmth of divine love when we are with our friends, family, co-workers, or fellow students.

Saint Paul implored the Thessalonians, "Do not quench the Spirit!" (1 Thess 5:19). He begged the Ephesians: "Do not grieve the Holy Spirit of God!" (Eph 4:30). How much we grieve the Holy Spirit when we limit the work he tries to accomplish in us, when we treat him as an unknown, or merely as a theological accessory, as something other than God's greatest gift.

A Plan of Life is an occasion for us to resolve to love the Holy Spirit by giving him free rein in our lives. That's the essence of the Christian life, which begins with God's grace. Docility to the Holy Spirit is what underlies all parts of the program of sanctification that we will be considering together and striving to put into practice.

CHAPTER 2

The Heroic Moment

Don't Hit That Snooze Button

The part of the Plan of Life that we will now consider may seem rather insignificant, but it's actually fundamental for growth in the spiritual life. It's temporally the first part of the ascetical program we need to implement each day. It's what Saint Josemaría Escrivá referred to as the "heroic minute," when we choose to get out of bed immediately as soon as our alarm sounds.

For many people using the adjective "heroic" for this moment in the day is very appropriate. Getting out of bed while we are still tired, when our limbs feel like they are weighed down by concrete, can seem like a superhuman feat. But the moment when our will is at its weakest, when every cell in our body screams for us to hit the snooze button, is exactly when we need to fight the battle to overcome one of our strongest bodily appetites and to start the day virtuously.

If we don't have the self-discipline to get out of bed, it will be difficult to live the disciplined life of a Christian disciple.

Several years ago, a teenager came to see me. He sincerely desired to prioritize prayer and grow in his faith in the midst of a demanding high school curriculum and many extra-curricular activities. Considering his schedule, he recognized that the best way for him to spend a half hour in daily meditation would be to get up an hour, rather than twenty minutes, before he needed to leave for school. But he struggled to find the strength to get out of bed on time. His perseverance eventually paid off, and once he began to pray in the morning, many other things in his life fell into place.

A young woman discerning religious life came to talk to me. She desired to make a holy hour and attend Mass each day. But because of the two jobs she was working to pay off college loans, she knew she would have to be up at 6:30 each morning. Many days, however, she was unable to get out of bed when her alarm clock rang, and as a result struggled to keep the rest of her life in order. But she kept working at it. Now she's a Sister of Life at a convent in Manhattan where I celebrate Mass frequently, wide awake and enthusiastic. The habit of the heroic moment has served her well!

A young, professional married woman with a great hunger to grow in faith also came to chat with me. She expressed her desire to pray for a half-hour in the morning and attend daily Mass. Her husband would leave for work about 5:00 am and her job began at 9:00 am. All she needed to do to get her spiritual life off to a great start each day was to stay up after seeing her husband off. She found it very difficult, however, to resist the temptation to return to bed and awaken a few hours later.

Eventually God helped her by giving her and her husband a new alarm clock—namely, a newborn—who gets them out of bed early whether they want to or not! Not long ago she told me that even with her added duties, the occasional chaos and the regular fatigue of being a mom, living the heroic moment at her son's behest, and using the time to pray as she's feeding him, has helped her discover an order that has made living the day with God unexpectedly easier.

The Plan of Life that leads to heroic virtue begins by valiantly living the first moment of the day.

Living the heroic moment effectively involves a few commonsense elements:

* *First*, set an appropriate wake-up time. If you are sleep deprived and try to get up earlier than you need to, it makes the heroic moment much harder.

* *Second*, live an analogous heroic moment at night. We need to get to bed on time in order to wake up rested. Watching comedy shows past midnight will only make responding to the alarm the next day more excruciating.

* *Third*, know and troubleshoot your vulnerabilities. Those who can't resist the snooze button need to put the alarm clock on the other side of the bedroom so they must get out of bed to shut it off. Some people also find it helpful to make their bed—or put water on their face—before silencing the alarm!

* *Lastly*, wake up out of love for God without exaggerating the difficulties. Anyone who has ever commuted in the early hours of the morning knows that many people get up early in the morning to drive to work. Some people energize themselves with copious amounts of coffee, but what is really getting them out of bed is their love for their families who depend on their work. Our love for God can inspire us in the same way.

CHAPTER 3

The Morning Offering

Start Your Day Off Right

In the previous chapter, we spoke about the heroic moment, the first element in a Plan of Life that trains us in holiness. Now I would like to turn to something we can do once we're out of bed: it's traditionally called the "Morning Offering."

The Morning Offering is a prayer in which we consecrate the day to God and ask his help to live it as a day of the Lord. It's normally best prayed when alert. For some, that can be as soon as they rise. For others, it is later, once they have had a cup of coffee or after they have showered. For those who set aside a period of time to pray each morning before the day gets going, it can be delayed until that time of prayer begins. The key is to pray the Morning Offering early, before news, e-mails, social media, or other tasks distract us.

The Morning Offering helps us to start the day focused on the purpose of time and the meaning of our life. Saint Paul wrote to the first Christians, "I appeal to you therefore, brothers and sisters, by the mercies of God, to present your bodies as a living sacrifice, holy and acceptable to God, which is your spiritual worship" (Rom 12:1). Those who make the Morning Offering begin the day by offering their body, mind, heart, soul, and strength to God. Saint Paul calls this our *logike latreia*, which means, "worship that is logical." And it does make sense for those seeking sanctity to make the whole day, from its outset, a holy and acceptable living sacrifice to God.

The Morning Offering can be long or short. It can be said in your own words or with prayers written by someone else. One of the shortest versions is simply to say *"Serviam!"* which means, "I will serve!" This commitment to serve God and others during the day is in direct opposition to the devil's attempts to get us to echo his own refusal to obey God, *"Non serviam!"*

Saint Philip Neri, the great sixteenth-century re-evangelizer of Rome, was a fan and promoter of a short, spontaneous Morning Offering. He would say, "Lord, today is the day I begin!" or on other occasions, "O Jesus, watch over me always, especially today, lest I betray you like Judas."

The Apostleship of Prayer, an organization founded in the nineteenth century in France to help Christians pray for the Church and the world, popularized a longer Morning Offering that has found its way into many prayer books:

O Jesus, through the Immaculate Heart of Mary, I offer you all my prayers, works, joys, and sufferings of this day, for the intentions of your Sacred Heart, in union with the holy Sacrifice of the Mass throughout the world, in reparation for my sins, for the intentions of my loved ones, and for the general intention recommended this month by the Holy Father.

In my own spiritual practice, I make the Morning Offering right after I've made the heroic moment. I kneel down at the side of my bed, face a crucifix, and pray sincerely in my own words. My personal Morning Offering incorporates the advice of both Saint John Vianney and Saint John Paul II.

Saint John Vianney, the patron saint of parish priests, counseled his parishioners to offer God each morning their entire selves —hearts, thoughts, words, actions—to use for his glory. He told them that they should renew the promises of their Baptism, thank their guardian angels, and petition God for all the graces needed for that day.

In his Morning Offering, John Paul II would consecrate the day to God through Mary by renewing the Marian consecration prayer of Saint Louis de Montfort from which his papal motto, *Totus Tuus* (Totally Yours), was taken. He also would pray for all those whom he would meet during the day, that he might receive them each as a gift and be for them a living sign of Christ's presence.

Following the lead of these two holy men, I generally make my Morning Offering along these lines:

> Thank you, Lord, for the gift of another day. Please help me to live it well. If it proves to be my last day on earth, help me to live it in total union with you so that it will be my first day in eternity. Grant me the graces I need to overcome all the temptations you know I'll face today. Awaken me to receive everyone the way I would receive you, and help me to be for them a reminder of you and your holy priesthood. Help me to make this day a liturgy of the hours, my heart an altar, and my work a commentary on the words of consecration. Into your hands, I commend this day, begging the intercession of my guardian angel and all the saints.

Saint Mechtilde, the famous thirteenth-century mystic, once shared that Jesus had revealed to her how pleased he is with the

Morning Offering. "When you awaken in the morning," she reported him to have said, "let your first act be to salute my heart, and to offer me your own." Jesus promised her that everyone who calls on his help at the beginning of the day would receive it.

The Morning Offering is a means by which you can build every new day on the rock of living faith in Christ. I encourage you to make this prayer a part of your daily spiritual game plan.

CHAPTER 4

The General Exam

End Your Day Well

In the last chapter we discussed how to get the Plan of Life off to a solid start each day by making a good Morning Offering, consecrating the day at its outset to God. Now I'd like to look at the spiritual practice that complements the Morning Offering at the end of the day: the "general examination of conscience" that saints and spiritual directors have long urged us to make in the evening before retiring.

The general exam is a prayerful daily evaluation that assesses our faithfulness to the consecration we made at the start of the day. When done well, it's one of the most powerful and important means to grow in the holiness that the Plan of Life is meant to foster.

In order to do a daily general exam well, however, we first need to make sure we don't confuse it with the examination of conscience we do before receiving the Sacrament of Penance. Unlike the examination of conscience, the general exam is not just a daily review of one's sins. Few people, after all, would be excited to end every day by pondering their moral failures! Instead, the general exam focuses on something much broader and deeper than a review of one's sins. It is centered on God: how he has sought to accompany us throughout the day, how much we've been conscious of that help, and how well we've responded.

Saint Bernard of Clairvaux, the great twelfth-century Doctor of the Church once wrote, "Strive to know yourself." The general exam is a crucial practice to grow in self-awareness in light of God's calling and grace. Saint John Vianney once told a businessman who had poor knowledge of his soul that his soul is more important than his company and that a daily accounting of his actions in conscience is more important than an audit of receipts and expenses.

If we're going to take our "moral bottom line" more seriously than a businessman takes his company's economic health, we should also consider making an examination of conscience every night. As accountants know, it is easier to make reconciliations on a daily basis rather than to wait a week, months, or even years.

Saint Ignatius of Loyola, the founder of the Society of Jesus, made the practice of the general exam (what he called the "examen") one of the pillars of the spiritual discipline he sought to impart to the men of his order as well as to the faithful. Ignatius advised doing the general exam twice a day, at noon and at bedtime. He believed it is essential to discern regularly the various movements of the soul, to determine which are from God, and to understand the direction God is trying to give our life.

Ignatius developed the traditional form of the general exam, which involves five parts:

1. Thank God for the gifts received throughout the day.

2. Ask God for the grace and the courage to know your sins and eradicate them.

3. Prayerfully review your thoughts, words, and actions throughout the day to determine where God has been present.

4. Beg God's mercy for your faults and ask his help to make the necessary changes to maintain better union with his saving love.

5. Resolve to amend your conduct with God's help.

For the last quarter century, I've made the daily general exam according to the advice given by Blessed Alvaro del Portillo. He encouraged people to review the whole day in light of how they've responded to God's presence. Ideally, this approach should lead to three prayerful responses: "Thank you, Lord," for the gift of so many graces over the course of the day; "Sorry," for the times I have failed to correspond to graces; and "Help me more," an expression of hope to do better the next day.

Socrates once said that an unexamined life is not worth living. The general exam is a means to avoid living an unexamined life. The general exam also strengthens us to resist the modern obsession with spontaneity and to live with intentionality, self-discipline, and joy. When we live the general exam faithfully, it helps us to heed the famous words of Psalm 95, "O that today you would listen to his voice! Do not harden your hearts" (vv. 7–8). Over time, the general exam helps us to become more sensitive and attentive to God's voice so we can find him in all our daily activities.

Like the Morning Offering, the general exam is a prayerful encounter with God that doesn't take very long, generally only a few minutes. But that short period of time is an investment in our relationship with God that will bear great fruit.

CHAPTER 5

Regular Prayer

The Most Important Conversation of Your Day

Saint John Paul II once said that "the art of prayer" is the one thing above all that should distinguish a Christian life focused on holiness. There's a lot of wisdom in that insight.

First, it indicates that prayer—which is an intimate, transformational dialogue with God, an exchange not just of words or even ideas but of persons—is *the most important part of a Plan of Life*, since every aspect of our Plan of Life should facilitate an encounter with God.

Second, Christian prayer is an art, not a technique. Prayer is not like engineering or chemistry, but more like playing or composing music. Inspiration is involved, namely the literal "in-breathing" that the Holy Spirit gives us, which is the basis of prayer. For, "we do not know how to pray as we ought, but that

very Spirit intercedes [for us] with sighs too deep for words"
(Rom 8:26).

Third, as Christians our life must be marked above all by
prayer. At our funeral, if we have truly lived a Christian life, the
mourners should easily be able to say that the most distinctive
thing about us was that we were a person of prayer! Our Christian
life is worth, basically, what our prayer is worth.

"Learning this Trinitarian shape of Christian prayer and living
it fully," Saint John Paul said, "is the secret of a truly vital Christianity." That's why daily prayer is so essential to becoming fully alive
spiritually. Without it, Saint John Paul II insisted, we would be at
risk of having our faith gradually weaken.

God wants prayer to fill our whole life. Our prayer life is not
meant to be a three-minute exercise before we go to bed or even a
three-hour exercise in a chapel. Prayer is the soul of our Christian
existence, the catalyst of a continual encounter with God that
helps us to be conscious of God's presence and remain in union
with his will throughout the entire day.

When saints and spiritual directors talk about prayer as part of
a Plan of Life, they mean fundamentally what Saint Teresa of Ávila
called "mental prayer," which describes the internal acts of our
mind and heart in meditation and contemplation. Mental prayer
is a time of silence in which we dialogue with God, listen for his
voice, ruminate on his words, seek his face, and allow ourselves to
be looked at with love. Saint Teresa described mental prayer as "a
close sharing between friends."

Mental prayer is not the same as vocal prayer, in which we
use words given to us from others—the Lord, saints, prayer
books—to converse with God. Vocal prayer is obviously good,
but it involves speaking to God more than listening interiorly to
what God wants to say. Prayer is more than merely "saying our

prayers," even if those prayers are the Lord's Prayer and the Hail Mary!

For most people, especially at the outset, mental prayer is not a switch we can just flip. It takes time to leave the daily noise of life behind to listen to God's gentle interior whispers.

Archbishop Fulton J. Sheen used to encourage a daily holy hour, or an hour of prayer, before the Lord in the Blessed Sacrament if possible. Saint Josemaría Escrivá used to urge lay people to split their prayer up into a half hour in the morning and a half hour in the evening, in order to keep the presence of God throughout the day. Those who struggle with incorporating prayer in their life can start with spending a solid block of ten to fifteen minutes of prayer a day and gradually build up to longer periods.

This may seem like a big commitment—and it is—but we also need to keep it in perspective. Most of us, if we had the opportunity to meet with the Holy Father or a great saint for a half hour each day, would enthusiastically jump at the chance. Mental prayer is an appointment with God himself, and if we don't jump at the chance to spend time with him, then it's probably a sign that God is not really yet God of our life.

Most of us have more time for prayer than we think. Even in the midst of busy schedules, we can usually find several things we can do without in order to carve out time for prayer. A recent Nielsen study found that the average American spends nearly thirty hours a week watching television. All most of us would need to do to find time to pray is to prioritize God over television. Do we love God enough to make time for him?

I generally try to set aside one prayer period first thing in the morning—before other distractions intervene—and then another period of prayer at night. I mark "Jesus" in my calendar and treat these appointments as the most important in my day, because they are. Some people may find that they can pray better at other times of the day when they are more alert and less distracted. The essential thing is not *when* we're praying but *that* we're praying.

Many people ask me how to do mental prayer well. There are lots of great books to explain mental prayer. I generally recommend Father Jacques Philippe's *Time for God* as an introduction. But at the same time—because prayer is an inspired art and not a technique—I just encourage people to make the time and begin, to ask the Lord to teach them how to pray, just as the first disciples did (see Lk 11:1).

Saint Josemaría once gave great advice to young students, "You don't know how to pray? Put yourself in the presence of God, and as soon as you have said, 'Lord, I don't know how to pray!' you can be sure you've already begun."

In fact, a few minutes of mental prayer right now most likely would please God more than reading the next chapter!

CHAPTER 6

Sacred Scripture

Live on God's Every Word

A person can't become a competent doctor or nurse without expert familiarity in human anatomy, nor could a good lawyer or judge without mastering law, nor a great athlete or referee without grasping a sport's rule book. By analogy, how likely is it, then, that we can become good Christians without regularly reading and understanding Sacred Scripture?

Saint Jerome, the great Father of the Church who translated the Bible from Greek and Hebrew into Latin, the common language of his fourth-century contemporaries, famously said, "Ignorance of Scripture is ignorance of Christ." To know Christ, we need to know Sacred Scripture: what Jesus said and did, what was foretold about him, how the Church and the Apostles put his words into practice. How can we know the Word-made-flesh unless we know the words he incarnated, fulfilled, and proclaimed?

That's why the Second Vatican Council exhorted the Christian faithful to read Scripture frequently. If we don't know Sacred Scripture, it's frankly a stretch to say we really know Jesus. And if we don't know Jesus well, it's obviously difficult to be his faithful followers and ardent apostles. That's why, as we ponder the various essential aspects of a Catholic Plan of Life, we need to highlight the essential pillar of familiarity with Sacred Scripture.

It's a scandal that so few Catholics truly know Sacred Scripture. A number of religious surveys have embarrassingly shown that average Protestants, Jews, and even atheists often know more about the Bible than average Catholics.

Like his predecessors, Pope Francis has been actively trying to get Catholics to become more familiar with the treasure trove of God's word. He has repeatedly appealed to Catholics to carry a tiny copy of the Gospels with them and read a part of it every day.

"Do you read a passage of the Gospel every day?" he asked the crowd present for his Sunday Angelus one day. "It is important!" he exclaimed. "It is a good thing to have a small book of the Gospel, a little one, and to carry it in our pocket or in our purse and read a little passage in whatever moment presents itself during the day."

As volunteers passed out copies of the Gospel in Saint Peter's Square, Pope Francis encouraged the crowd, "Let the Gospel be with us always, because it is the word of Jesus in order for us to be able to listen to him."

There can't be a missionary transformation of the Church— something Pope Francis has made a priority in his papacy—unless Catholics know Sacred Scripture well enough to live it and share it with others. Unless Catholics really know Christ, we cannot preach him effectively, and one of the primary ways to know Christ is to know him through Scripture.

Several years ago, I had what turned out to be an important conversion in an airport. Upon seeing another priest in the security lane, we decided to grab lunch. When the cashier asked if there would be one bill or two, I said, "One," and gave my credit card.

Father Bob replied, "The Book of Sirach says we should go dutch!"

I quickly retorted, "The Last Supper wasn't a dutch treat and Jesus calls us to love as he loves!" Then I picked up the bill.

When we got to the table, I just had to ask whether he had made up the quotation from Sirach.

"Not at all!" he said as he opened a worn Bible and pointed out the verse that recommends sharing the expenses of a business or journey (see Sir 42:3).

I asked my new priest friend how he knew Sacred Scripture so well. He said he had made a promise on the day of his ordination to read the entire Bible once a year and that he had been faithful to that promise.

"After twenty-four years," he said with a smile, "you get to know what Sirach says about restaurant bills!"

He then went on to tell me that it takes only twelve to fifteen minutes each day to read the whole Bible each year, and that there are various apps and books that make the endeavor easier. After lunch, I bid the priest goodbye and left with a renewed commitment to read Scripture and incorporate it into my daily schedule.

Not everyone can read the entire Bible every year, but reading Scripture regularly is something every Catholic who takes the faith seriously can and ought to do. If we are already setting aside time for mental prayer every day as the last chapter encourages, then Scripture can serve as a springboard for that prayer time. At the beginning of a prayer period, one can read a passage from Scripture or the Gospel reading of the day and let the word of God inspire the time of mental prayer.

Wouldn't it be a beautiful thing if every Catholic would spend just a few minutes a day getting to know the Lord through Sacred Scripture?

Jesus told us that we don't live on bread alone, "but by every word that comes from the mouth of God" (Mt 4:4). To live a Plan of Life that helps us to grow in union with Christ, we need a regular diet of Sacred Scripture. The word of God is a powerful source of nourishment for our spiritual lives. It's one of the secrets to spiritual health in this world—and it prepares us for the celestial banquet that will know no end.

CHAPTER 7

Weekly Little Easter

Sunday Mass and the Christian Sabbath

We cannot become saints without Sunday Mass. The greatest of all the graces God gives us to make us holy is the Mass. In the Mass, God unites himself to us in Holy Communion. How can we fail to grow in sanctity when we hunger for and actually enter into existential communion with him who is "holy, holy, holy"?

The Second Vatican Council's *Dogmatic Constitution on the Church* (*Lumen Gentium*) described the Mass as the "source and summit of the whole Christian life," which means it's the starting point from which everything flows and the goal toward which everything is meant to be directed. A truly Christian life finds in the Eucharist its font and apex. Christian life, in short, is a eucharistic life.

We'll have a chance later to examine more deeply the role of the Eucharist in our Plan of Life, but it's important for us to recognize now that living Sunday well is crucial for reasons that go beyond how it brings us into sacramental contact with the Lord. The way we live Sunday is crucial to our *whole approach* to faith, time, work, rest, charity, and our Christian identity.

First, living Sunday well orients our whole approach to the faith. The early Christians used to call Sunday "little Easter," because they lived it as a weekly, joy-filled celebration of the Lord's Resurrection. To them, Mass wasn't simply a religious duty to be checked off a to-do list. Sunday was an occasion to rejoice in the real fulcrum of human history: that Jesus Christ has risen from the dead and is still very much alive, he accompanies us and helps us to live life to the full. The early Church changed the Sabbath from the seventh day to the first day of the week to mark this new center of history.

One of the principal reasons so many of the Pharisees, Herodians, Sadducees, and others conspired to have Jesus killed was because of his behavior on the Sabbath. Jesus healed multiple people on the Sabbath. He allowed his Apostles to do the minimal work of picking heads of grain to eat on the Sabbath. This scandalized the scribes and the Pharisees, who taught that no one should do any work at all on the Sabbath, even works of charity (as if loving a neighbor or feeding the hungry would ever be offensive to God). Jesus was willing to die for the meaning of the Sabbath, and if it was so important to him, it ought to be similarly important to us.

Jesus taught that the Sabbath was put in place for our well being, not the other way around (see Mk 2:27). In other words, Sunday is ultimately a gift to renew us in the image of God who, as the Book of Genesis tells us, rested on the Sabbath and rejoiced in creation (see Gen 2:3). The Sabbath allows us to rejoice also in the wonder of God's creation and, even more, in our more wondrous re-creation or salvation in Christ.

When we truly live the Sabbath as a day of rest, it restores our proper attitude toward work, ensuring that we don't become enslaved to work or make an idol of the material things it can provide. God pointed out the potential for enslavement to our work when he gave us the commandment to keep holy the Lord's day:

> Remember that you were a slave in the land of Egypt, and the LORD your God brought you out from there with a mighty hand and an outstretched arm; therefore the LORD your God commanded you to keep the sabbath day. (Deut 5:15)

The Sabbath is a weekly "exodus" from the daily routine of our lives that is meant to liberate us from all types of interior slavery so that we may love God and others.

The scribes and Pharisees had forgotten the true meaning of the Sabbath, which is why Jesus vigorously opposed them on it. The Sabbath had become a day of slavery; those in authority laid unbearable burdens on others without lifting a finger to move them (see Mt 23:4). The day had become an end in itself rather than a day made for man, to free him from slavery to the burdens of daily life. By his words and actions, Jesus brought back the Sabbath's original meaning: to rescue man from slavery to his material needs, worries, and sins. Man is freed so that he can put God first, rediscover his dignity with respect to social and economic life, and through faith achieve his destiny by giving himself back to God.

I think one of the reasons so many people today are bewildered and depressed is because they've lost faith in the gift of the Sabbath. The majority of Catholics in the United States don't go to Mass every week. But even among those who do, some still view their Sunday Mass obligation as merely a duty to get out of the way. For many, Sunday has become just an extension of the weekend, a day for diversion rather than conversion, a time to watch athletes compete for fleeting championships rather than to be refreshed in the midst of our own marathon toward an imperishable crown. That's why living Sunday well—the whole of Sunday —is so important in a Plan of Life.

Jesus is our model in everything, and so he shows us how to keep the Lord's Day holy. On the Sabbath, Jesus proclaimed the Good News, freed captives, and healed those in need. His example provides an examination of conscience for us. The Sabbath is not about our personal life or even just our relationship with Jesus in the restricted sense. The Sabbath is also about bringing Jesus, his good news, and the healing power of his love and mercy to others. It's a chance to spend time with family members, to visit and assist those who might be alone, and to carry out some of the corporal and spiritual works of mercy.

Describing the importance of the Lord's Day, Saint John Paul II once wrote:

> From the Sunday Mass there flows a tide of charity destined to spread into the whole life of the faithful, beginning by inspiring the very way in which they live the rest of Sunday. If Sunday is a day of joy, Christians should declare by their actual behavior that we cannot be happy "on our own." They look around to find people who may need their help. It may be that in their neighborhood or among those they know there are sick people, elderly people, children, or immigrants who precisely on Sundays feel more keenly their isolation, needs, and suffering.

Lastly, living Sunday well is essential to strengthening our bond as Christians, especially as the number of Christians dwindles in some areas of the world and communities become more prone to dispersion, misunderstanding, and persecution. Celebrating our weekly little Easter together—not only liturgically but also in communal activities—strengthens us in our Christian identity. When we live Sunday well, we find others who can support us in our Plan of Life and we can support them in theirs.

Sunday is the time when each of us should exclaim:

This is the day that the LORD has made;
    let us rejoice and be glad in it! (Ps 118:24)

It is not hard to keep the Sabbath holy when we live the radical joy that lies at the heart of it!

CHAPTER 8

Frequent Confession

Your Sins Are Forgiven

Our focus on the importance of the Christian Sabbath connects to another essential aspect of a Catholic Plan of Life: the Sacrament of Penance or Reconciliation. Jesus established this sacrament not just on a Sunday, but on Easter Sunday night! He came to save us from eternal death—and on the day he rose from the dead he established the sacrament that remedies what causes eternal death, namely, unrepented and unforgiven sin.

Let me explain. When Jesus entered the Upper Room on Easter Sunday, the first thing he did was wish the Apostles "peace," the *definitive* peace between God and humanity that comes through the forgiveness of sins. Then Jesus said, "As the Father has sent me, so I send you" (Jn 20:21). And we know that the Father sent Jesus as the Lamb of God to take away the sins of the world. Finally, he breathed on the Apostles the power of the Holy Spirit—because only God can forgive sins—and said,

"Receive the Holy Spirit. If you forgive the sins of any, they are forgiven them; if you retain the sins of any, they are retained" (Jn 20:22–23). And since the Apostles didn't receive from Jesus the ability to read everyone's soul and heart, the only way they would know which sins to forgive and which not to pardon would be if people told them their sins. Those are the essential elements of the Sacrament of Penance.

Jesus clearly thought that the Sacrament of Penance was important enough to establish it almost immediately when he rose from the dead. If the forgiveness of sins is so central to the mystery of our redemption, it's unsurprising then that the devil does everything he can to persuade people *not* to go to confession. Some people are duped into believing that they're as sinless as the Blessed Virgin Mary or that they just commit *peccadilloes* that don't need to be confessed and pardoned. Others know they are sinners but are convinced they can confess their sins "directly to God." But if the Son of God established the Sacrament of Penance on Easter, then it would seem that he would want us to take advantage of it!

The Church asks that all Catholics go to confession at least once a year, but we should never treat the Church's minimal requirement as the maximum. In fact, the Church has routinely recommended that we receive the Sacrament of Penance more frequently. "Without being strictly necessary," the *Catechism of the Catholic Church* says, "confession of everyday faults (venial sins) is nevertheless strongly recommended by the Church" (1458). The *Catechism* stresses confession of venial sins because it presumes that if we have committed a mortal sin, we would go to confession immediately. But the unfortunate reality is that if someone is not going to confession regularly, he or she may wait for months to confess even mortal sins.

Pope Francis has said on numerous occasions that he goes to confession every two weeks, because "the pope, too, is a sinner." Saint John Paul II went every week. Pope Pius XII went every day. This is not—we can be certain—because the popes are clandestine serial killers, blasphemers, liars, thieves, or regularly commit other mortal sins. Rather, they have recognized what so many saints have known: that the Sacrament of Penance is one of the greatest means of spiritual growth that Christ has given us. The more we sincerely examine our conscience, contritely confess our sins, and perseveringly resolve to amend our lives, the more we recognize sinful patterns in our lives and receive the grace from God to resolve them.

What are the fruits of frequent confession? The *Catechism* lists several of them:

> The regular confession of our venial sins helps us form our conscience, fight against evil tendencies, let ourselves be healed by Christ, and progress in the life of the Spirit. By receiving more frequently through this sacrament the gift of the Father's mercy, we are spurred to be merciful as he is merciful. (1458)

Pope Pius XII gave a more extended list of the spiritual advantages in his 1943 encyclical *On the Mystical Body of Christ* (*Mystici Corporis Christi*):

> By [frequent confession] genuine self-knowledge is increased, Christian humility grows, bad habits are corrected, spiritual neglect and tepidity are resisted, the conscience is purified, the will strengthened, a salutary self-control is attained, and grace is increased in virtue of the sacrament itself.

Let's briefly examine the eight benefits Pope Pius XII named.

⸎ *Increase in genuine self-knowledge*: Regular, thorough, courageous examination of our conscience helps us to be honest in appraising our behaviors, character, and

movements of the soul. It allows us to know ourselves—
both the good and the ugly—in God's light.

❖ *Growth in Christian humility*: Humility begins with
seeing ourselves as we really are, but then extends to
relating reverently to God and others as they really are.

❖ *Correction of bad habits*: We all have bad habits, but few of
us fight intelligently to correct them. Frequent confession
helps us to identify our vices, probe their root causes with
God's assistance, and come up with a game plan to battle
against and eradicate them.

❖ *Resistance of spiritual neglect and tepidity*: Pope Benedict
XVI once said:

> The greatest danger for a Christian [is] not that he says
> no, but a very tepid yes. This tepidness really discredits
> Christianity. Faith must become in us the flame of love,
> a flame that truly ignites my being, becomes the great
> passion of my being, and so ignites my neighbor.

Frequent reception of God's mercy fills us with the flame
of his love and burns away spiritual dross.

❖ *Purification of the conscience*: To keep our inner life attuned
to God, we must not only regularly calibrate it through
examination of our actions, but we also need to receive the
sacramental help God gives. To follow an unpurified
conscience is as wise as trying to drive with a windshield
obscured by dirt.

❖ *Strengthening of the will*: A strong will perseveres in doing
what is right and in saying to God, "your will be done"
(Mt 6:10). Our failures and falls discourage us and weaken
the will, but God's mercy picks us up and inspires us to
keep fighting.

❧ *Attainment of self-control*: To be Jesus' disciple, we have to deny ourselves, pick up our cross, and follow him. Frequent confession helps us to control our selfishness and discipline our appetites.

❧ *Increase of grace in virtue of the sacrament itself*: Grace is our participation as creatures in the very life and love of God. The sacraments give the grace they signify and the Sacrament of Penance helps us to live in the truly awe-inspiring, life-changing reality of God's merciful love.

If we really want to grow in holiness, how could we neglect these fruits of frequent confession? Frequent confession helps us never to tire of receiving the love and mercy God wants to lavish on us.

CHAPTER 9

Eucharistic Adoration

Crush Your Idols

During my time as executive editor of *The Anchor*, the weekly newspaper of the Diocese of Fall River in Massachusetts, I always had a mischievous desire to run a huge front-page story, "Jesus Christ Comes to the Diocese!" And, just as we would have if the pope were coming, the newspaper would feature how Jesus comes to the parishes of the diocese every day and takes up residence in tabernacles and monstrances. Although I never acted on that desire, every week we proudly had a special feature that listed the opportunities for adoration all over the diocese.

One of the real movements of the Holy Spirit in recent times has been to encourage many Catholic parishes, pastors, and parishioners to create opportunities for eucharistic adoration. These happy developments give us the opportunity to turn to something that ought to be part of a Catholic's Plan of Life each week: a holy hour in the presence of the Lord Jesus in the Holy Eucharist.

For some time, the popes have explicitly encouraged eucharistic adoration. During his pontificate, Pope Benedict XVI heartily recommended the practice to pastors and lay people, both individually and in community.

Pope Francis has said that eucharistic adoration is his favorite type of prayer. In an interview, he shared that he spends an hour beginning at seven o'clock in the evening before the Blessed Sacrament. He has preached that the sign of a Christian truly focused on Jesus "is adoration of Jesus," and he noted how adoration either crushes or exposes our idolatries, because as human beings if we do not take time to adore God, we will end up adoring people and things.

The idols in our life can be revealed by the excuses we give when we don't make time to be with Jesus in the Blessed Sacrament. For some people, it's work or family or chores. For others, it's television or exercise. For others, it's time with friends. But, if over the course of the 168 hours in a week that God gives us, we can't find one to come to praise and thank him, we can be pretty sure we're placing something or someone else before him.

When I was in college, I was part of a group that started eucharistic adoration on First Friday. I still remember trying to get some of my Catholic friends to sign up for an hour; many were reluctant to commit themselves even to a monthly obligation.

"If the pope wanted to have a conversation with you about your life for one hour a month," I asked some of them, "would you keep that appointment?" When they would nod affirmatively, I would reply, "Well, how about an appointment with the pope's boss?"

To those guys who had girlfriends, I'd ask, "How hard is it for you to set and keep a date with your girlfriend?"

"Not very," they'd reply with a grin.

Then I'd ask, "Well, do you love Jesus enough to make and keep a 'date' with him once a month?"

If we believe that Jesus is truly present in the Blessed Sacrament, and if we really love him, then going to adore him is as much a no-brainer as two people in love who want to spend time together.

In terms of a commitment for a Plan of Life, I recommend a eucharistic holy hour once a week. It might be best to choose a fixed time so that, barring true emergencies, nothing else will tempt us to miss our "date with Jesus." Mark "Jesus" in your calendar just as you would write down any other important appointment —and then keep it.

One of my greatest joys as a parish priest has been to see transformation happen in my parishioners when they begin to respond to Jesus' Holy Thursday request, "Could you not stay awake with me one hour?" (Mt 26:40). I still get thank-you notes from parishioners who took up this challenge and who tell me several years later about the difference it has made in their lives.

If you're not already regularly spending time with Jesus in the Eucharist, I urge you to make a resolution to do so as part of your Plan of Life.

CHAPTER 10

Charity and Almsgiving

Live Christ-like Compassion

Jesus came from heaven to earth to form us to be children of God. He told us to love others as he has loved us, and he wants to help us to do so. Jesus, the Good Samaritan, wants to train us to become good Samaritans. The kingdom he established is one in which we take responsibility for each other as our brothers' keepers. The Lord and Master entered into our world not to be served but to serve and to teach us to become great through service. This is the theological foundation for Christian charity. Jesus exhorts us as Christians:

> Whenever you give alms, do not sound a trumpet before you, as the hypocrites do in the synagogues and in the streets, so that they may be praised by others ... do not let your left hand know what your right hand is doing, so that your alms may be done in secret; and your Father who sees in secret will reward you. (Mt 6:2–4)

Pope Francis once wrote, "In each of our neighbors, we must see a brother or sister for whom Christ died and rose again. What we ourselves have received, we have received for them as well."

Saint John Vianney made a similar point to the Christians of his day. "Your well-being," he stated in a catechesis, "is nothing other than a depository that God has placed in your hands."

The word "almsgiving" comes from the Greek word *eleēmosynē* for mercy and relates to the phrase we say in Mass, *Kyrie, eleison*, "Lord, have mercy." Almsgiving refers principally not to the giving of goods to the indigent, but to the Christ-like compassion that leads us to do all we can for those in need. Of course, there's an obvious material dimension to giving alms, since many suffer from various forms of material need. Genuinely sacrificing our money and possessions—giving not just a little but giving to the point that we ourselves go without something we need—is one of the greatest ways to ensure that we don't worship money, the ancient golden calf. Many of us are tempted to place our faith, hope, and love in mammon instead of God. Our spiritual growth is impeded because we, like the rich young man in the parable, won't give what we have to the poor to follow Christ more fully (see Mt 19:16–30).

Notice, however, that the Gospel doesn't list many material benefactions of Jesus. His principal alms was the gift of himself. On various occasions, the evangelists say that his "heart was moved with pity," and as a result he taught, healed, fed, forgave, and resuscitated (see Mk 6:34). Almsgiving, therefore, involves all of the works of mercy, not just giving food to the hungry, clothing to the naked, and welcome to strangers, but also such things as visiting the sick and imprisoned, teaching and counseling those in need, forgiving and calling people out of sin, and praying perseveringly for the living and the dead.

Many of the people who come to see me for spiritual direction live according to a vow or promise of poverty, and so their almsgiving can seldom take on the form of giving money or possessions. Instead, I encourage them to give of themselves and their time. They can reach out to care for someone in need, pray for that person, visit, make a phone call, write a letter or an e-mail. Those who try this, for even just fifteen minutes a day, have learned that charity often doesn't stop at the quarter-hour, but begins to mushroom into more.

This leads us to an important truth: in a Plan of Life, the key is to *plan* our charity. Random acts of kindness ought to be encouraged, but they are not enough. Just as prayer ought to be scheduled rather than remain entirely spontaneous, the same goes for charity. It's not sufficient to wait for someone in need to come to us. We know people are suffering and that Jesus personally identifies with them (see Mt 25:31–46). So we need to go out in search of them. We need to plan. Charity is too important in the Christian life to remain a matter of happenstance. Christ's charity toward us, after all, was planned from before the foundation of the world.

We're summoned by God to plan and to grow our charity more than a business owner seeks growth in profits. In this way, we will grow in the image of the Divine Giver, which is the purpose of a Plan of Life.

CHAPTER 11

Holy Week

Enter the Center of History

It always startles me when people, at the end of Palm Sunday Mass, politely say, "See you next Sunday," meaning, on Easter. The celebrations of Holy Week are just not on some peoples' radars, and this is an extraordinary spiritual loss!

Occasionally I've been asked, "Why aren't Holy Thursday, Good Friday, and the Easter Vigil considered holy days of obligation?" I think we are not obligated to attend these liturgies for the same reason there are no laws mandating the celebration of a loved one's birthday: it would be unfathomable that such a law would be needed!

For disciples of Jesus to forget the principal celebrations of our faith is as incomprehensible as a Red Sox fan who doesn't watch the World Series when the Sox are playing.

Of course, some of us are not able to make it to all of the liturgies of Holy Week due to work or family responsibilities or to living in areas where there are not enough priests to make it possible to celebrate all of them. Even if you are unable to attend all of the Holy Week liturgies, however, there are ways to observe the solemn nature of the week: by following the daily readings, fitting in more prayer time, and trying to make it to as many of the liturgies as possible.

Regardless of other commitments, Holy Week ought to be our most faith-filled week of the year.

Holy Week is holy because of all Jesus Christ did during this week. From his triumphal entry into Jerusalem on Palm Sunday, to his teaching in the Temple, to the Last Supper, to his prayer in Gethsemane, to his arrest, torture, crucifixion, preaching, and death on Good Friday, to his rest in the tomb and his glorious Resurrection on the third day, this week contains the central events of our faith.

But Holy Week is also holy because it's supposed to make *us* holy—if we follow Jesus closely, if we enter into these mysteries, if we receive within us all he won for us during this time. The liturgies in which we remember the pivotal events of Jesus' life are full of abundant graces for all Christians.

On Holy Thursday, at the beginning of that most precious meal of all time, Jesus said to the Apostles, "I have eagerly desired to eat this Passover with you before I suffer" (Lk 22:15). Jesus says the same thing to us: with great eagerness he wants to eat his Passover with us. The opportunity to enter into the celebration of the Last Supper is the most important dinner invitation we have ever received. On Holy Thursday, we celebrate the institution of the Eucharist and the priesthood that makes that perpetual gift possible. Could we possibly have a more important invitation on Holy Thursday night?

If there's ever one day during the year on which every Christian should think about taking a personal day, it's Good Friday. Most of us would naturally take time off work or school to be with a dying family member. We should make a similar effort to try to be with Jesus on Good Friday. If we went back in time and were present in Jerusalem on the day Jesus died, would we have wanted to be with him, as Mary and the other faithful disciples were, or would we have been busy about other—probably far less important —matters?

The Easter Vigil is by far the most important and beautiful Mass of the entire year, in which we thank God for the supreme gift of his Resurrection and reflect on what it means for the world. There are Masses on Easter morning that certainly fulfill our obligation, but the Easter Vigil is truly a special event. On this night, we enter with faith into all the central events of salvation history, meditate on how they're all fulfilled in Christ, and rejoice at the new life God gives us. It's the most important and beautiful liturgy in Catholicism. This Mass in particular has the power to change us as we celebrate it because it pushes us to the liturgical limit in expressing our love and gratitude to God for our salvation.

Holy Week is the week that contains within it the power to make us holy. For those living a Plan of Life geared toward training in holiness, this week ought to be circled months in advance on the calendar and lived with prayerful intensity and profound joy!

CHAPTER 12

The Rosary

Enroll in the School of Mary

After Jesus himself, the greatest model and master of the Christian spiritual life is the Blessed Virgin Mary, whose contemplative heart pondered, treasured, and integrated the Lord's word and action. Like pieces of a precious and beautiful mosaic, Mary "treasured all these words and pondered them in her heart" (Lk 2:19). To live a Plan of Life, we do well to enter into Mary's school just like the first disciples in the Upper Room before Pentecost.

The Rosary is one of the greatest means by which we enter into Mary's school and learn from her how to stay united with her Son. The tradition of the Church, many saints, and numerous popes all agree that the best way to enroll in Mary's academy of holiness is through praying the Rosary. Therefore, it's fitting to focus on this greatest of all Marian devotions as a crucial part of our spiritual game plan.

Praying three Rosaries a day has been part of Pope Francis' daily Plan of Life for many years. His approach to the Rosary changed when, as a priest, he witnessed Saint John Paul II on his knees publicly leading the faithful in the prayer of the Rosary. He saw in this holy man the fruits of Marian devotion and sought to follow Saint John Paul II's example.

In the beautiful exhortation *On the Most Holy Rosary* (*Rosarium Virginis Mariae*), Saint John Paul II called the Rosary the "echo of the prayer of Mary," a "'compendium' of the Gospel," and something that, "reclaimed in its full meaning, goes to the heart of the Christian life." It's a prayer, he said, that helps us enter Mary's contemplative heart and ponder the joyful, luminous, sorrowful and glorious moments in the life of the "blessed fruit of [Mary's] womb." The Rosary also brings the joyful, luminous, sorrowful, and glorious rhythm of our own life into harmony with God's life.

My earliest childhood memories are of praying the Rosary with my family at the kitchen table. This family tradition taught me that God was real and part of our daily life. It also taught me how important daily prayer was, with others, for others, and mutually strengthened by others. It deeply nourished my priestly vocation. I've continued to pray the Rosary regularly until this day. But that doesn't mean praying it has always been easy. It also doesn't mean that I've always prayed it as well as I would have wished. In college and seminary, I would generally pray it silently as I walked to class. Now I often pray it in the car or walking on the streets of Manhattan. When I pray it at the end of the day, I normally stand or pace to stay awake. Just like any prayer, it's sometimes a battle to fight off distractions or occasional boredom even as we are contemplating the mysteries of Christ's life.

It's worth it, however. As with physical exercise, the effort and the repetition pay off. One may not set a record on any given day at the track or the gym, but the cumulated impact of exercising each day makes athletic achievement possible later. With the Rosary, some days we just get through it the best we can, but that hard work makes it possible to receive deeper fruits of prayer later when prayer is not so arduous.

I've found praying the Rosary each day to be the greatest aid to help me overcome the temptation to pray only when it is convenient. The structure of the Rosary, its duration, and its mysteries, train us in persevering prayer that serves us in every aspect of the Plan of Life.

I've always been moved that in Michelangelo's famous Last Judgment in the Sistine Chapel, the "lifeline" that the angels hold out to lift people to heaven is a set of Rosary beads. The Rosary is a chain of love linking us to contemplate Christ so that we may behold him forever. It's a chain of love that links us to Mary so that through her intercession, we may come to reverence and love Christ and our neighbor as she did. It's a chain of love Mary holds out to everyone seeking to live by a Plan of Life.

Time Out

By this point, you might be tempted to feel overwhelmed by the various practices we've discussed. Resist the temptation!

Sometimes when we're introduced to living a Plan of Life, we can see it as a series of independent religious exercises that build up different spiritual muscle groups. But a Plan of Life is much more than discrete prayers and practices: it's a cohesive whole that forms us to live consciously and continuously in God's presence.

That's the key: striving to encounter God in each of the parts of the Plan of Life in such a way that we begin gradually to share more and more of each day with God. As with anything in life, we must crawl, walk, and occasionally trip before we can run. The key is to keep moving in the right direction.

What we've considered until now are some of the most significant of the regular encounters that God wants to have with us. They're the foundation for living with God.

Before moving on to the next part of the book, perhaps it would be good to pause and prayerfully consider what you have read so far so that the Plan of Life does not remain just a wish, but becomes a resolution.

Some questions may be helpful:

1. Which parts of the Plan of Life discussed so far are you already living well?

_____

_____

_____

_____

Which are you doing but need improvement?

_____

_____

_____

_____

Which are you not doing at all or have never even considered?

_____

_____

_____

_____

2. Of the practices in need of improvement, which do you sense God would be most pleased to have you work on first?

_____

_____

_____

What do you think it will take for you, with God's help, to make that step?

_____

_____

_____

_____

How will you monitor your progress and continue to improve?

_____

_____

_____

_____

3. Of the parts of a Plan of Life you have not yet lived at all, which do you think would be the easiest to start with?

_____

_____

_____

_____

The most important to start with?

_____

_____

_____

_____

Knowing yourself, which practice do you think would be best for you to choose to incorporate into your life first?

_____

_____

_____

_____

4. Who are the people in your life who can help you stay motivated to begin living by a Plan of Life and check on your progress?

_____

_____

_____

_____

BEYOND
THE BASICS

CHAPTER 13

Eucharistic Practices

Nourishment for the Journey

Daily Mass: The Secret Elevator to Holiness

Sometimes we can think that the pursuit of sanctity involves all the things we need to do on our end to grow in holiness. But whenever God calls us to anything, he always provides the means to achieve it. Growth in holiness is not about our work, as if we were laboring up a 10,000-step staircase to heaven. To use Saint Thérèse of Lisieux's famous image, growing in holiness is more like an elevator trip with God who takes us for a ride to the top. One such "elevator" that helps us make leaps and bounds in the spiritual life is daily Mass.

During the fourth century in the town of Abitene in northern Africa, forty-nine Christians were warned that if they convened on Sunday they would, under orders of Emperor Diocletian, be arrested, tried, and executed. They still all showed up. When the pro-consul Anullinus asked why they risked their lives to worship, one of them, Emeritus, famously replied, "*Sine dominico non possumus*," or loosely translated, "Without the Lord on Sunday, we can't make it."

The Abitinian martyrs preferred to die physically and keep their spiritual bond with Jesus in the Eucharist rather than to live physically and not maintain that communion. Their witness leads us to ask ourselves some very direct questions. Can I live without Jesus in the Eucharist? Is communion with Jesus in the Eucharist the real fulcrum of my life or just a holy accessory? And if communion with Jesus is the root and center of my life, can I really go six out of seven days a week without receiving him?

I remember very well when this question struck me with all its practical consequences. It was September of my freshman year in college. Living on my own for the first time, I began to wonder what my priorities should be and what role God should play in my life moving forward. I knew that I wanted God to be God: not just part of my life, but Lord.

That led to the question: "If God is really God in my life, and if he comes down each day from heaven to altars all over the earth, how can I not make him the God of my Monday, Tuesday, Wednesday, Thursday, Friday, and Saturday?" I realized that if I really believed that the Eucharist was Jesus Christ, then I should make every effort to receive him more frequently. The next day I went to daily Mass. And with God's help, I have persevered in going to Mass every day of my life since. That's been the greatest gift of my life, and I don't know where I would be without this daily gift of gifts!

We pray in the Our Father, "Give us this day our daily bread" (Mt 6:11). The Greek word *epiousios*, often translated as "daily," is a word that has captivated saints and scholars for centuries. It only appears twice in the New Testament and nowhere else in ancient Greek literature. The word has also been variously translated as "super-substantial" and "necessary for existence." The early Church Fathers interpreted this mysterious word to refer to the Eucharist. Just as God rained down manna for the Jews each day in the desert, so he gives us each day the "super-substantial" bread of his Son to nourish us on our pilgrimage to the eternal promised land.

When God answers our prayers to give us his Son each day, how do we respond?

The patron saint of priests, Saint John Vianney, used to do everything he could to "upgrade" the eucharistic practice of his parishioners from weekly communicants to daily. He tried to encourage them to frequent daily Mass so that Jesus could do his sanctifying work. He once lamented that if his parishioners would receive Jesus in the Eucharist more often, they would not merely remain "good," but would become saints! The truth is that if we, too, were to receive Jesus more often in the Eucharist and with greater purity, love, and devotion, we would become holier, too!

Of course, it's not always possible for everyone to go to Mass every day, because of work, school, and other responsibilities. In certain areas, it can also be difficult to find a daily Mass at all or one scheduled at a time that fits into the day for those who work. But every Catholic who seeks to grow in holiness should have a hunger to receive Jesus every day and make an effort to attend daily Mass when possible.

If you are unable to make it to daily Mass, you can always watch Mass online or on TV. You can also make a spiritual communion (a spiritual practice we'll discuss next). Regardless, we should all be striving to live more intentionally a truly eucharistic life, which is a truly Christian life.

Spiritual Communion: Stoke Your Eucharistic Hunger

For those who, for whatever reason, find themselves unable to attend Mass daily, spiritual communions will be essential for growth in holiness. This spiritual practice is also key for those who do have the ability to attend each day, because it can help us attend Mass with greater awareness, awe, and adoration.

A few years after my priestly ordination, I was sent to a parish where, on my first day there, I celebrated the noon Mass. The number of Mass goers so impressed me—it was like a Sunday Mass crowd—that, before the final blessing, I thanked the attendees for their inspiring faith and love for Jesus in the Holy Eucharist. After Mass, a curmudgeonly woman stopped to see me in the sacristy.

"Father Landry," she said, "I think I'm going to like you because you seem to be smart and have a lot of energy. But I think I owe it to you to disabuse you of your naïveté. Many of us seniors are here not so much because we love Jesus—although it was kind of you to think so—but because we're bored and don't have anything else to do with our time!"

I soon discovered that this woman's comment did not reflect the thought of the vast majority of attendees. Yet it did reveal that even if we are going to Mass daily, lukewarmness can creep into our spiritual lives. And this is where spiritual communions are helpful; they can prevent routine from stealing the awe we should have for Jesus' presence in the Eucharist. In a spiritual communion, we ask the Lord to come abide in us the way he would if we were to receive him in Holy Communion. We express our desire to receive and lovingly embrace him.

The most famous and popular vocal prayer for a spiritual communion was written by Saint Alphonsus Ligouri in the eighteenth century:

My Jesus, I believe that you are present in the Most Holy Sacrament. I love you above all things and I desire to receive you into my soul. Since I cannot at this moment receive you sacramentally, come at least spiritually into my heart. I embrace you as if you were already there and unite myself wholly to you. Never permit me to be separated from you. Amen.

The one I pray most often was written by nineteenth-century priests in Spain and popularized later by Saint Josemaría Escrivá. "I wish, my Lord, to receive you with the purity, humility, and devotion with which your most holy Mother received you, with the spirit and fervor of all the saints." Before saying "all the saints" in this prayer, I'll often add a specific invocation to the saint the Church is celebrating that day, the patron saint of the parish, or to a particular saint for a particular intention.

We can also use expressions from Sacred Scripture or some of the great eucharistic hymns to make a spiritual communion:

⁂ "Sir, give us this bread always," as the people in the Capernaum synagogue said to Jesus (Jn 6:34);

⁂ "Give us this day our daily bread" (Mt 6:11);

⁂ "Stay with us, [Lord]!" as the two disciples said to Jesus in Emmaus (Lk 24:29);

⁂ "*O res mirabilis*" ("O wondrous reality!");

⁂ "*Fac me tibi semper magis credere, in te spem habere, te diligere*," ("Make me always believe more in you, hope in you, and love you!") taken respectively from Saint Thomas Aquinas' *Panis Angelicus*, and *Adoro Te Devote*.

We can also make spiritual communions in our own words. There are many ways to incorporate spiritual communions into our daily lives. We can pray spiritual communions when making visits to the Blessed Sacrament or at eucharistic adoration. Homebound parishioners can make a spiritual communion when they cannot come to Mass, but are able to watch it on television. One can pray a spiritual communion before Mass to help bring about a more conscious, active, fruitful, and passionate participation in the sacred liturgy.

Spiritual communions are such a short, simple practice that we can easily incorporate several into our day. I often pray a spiritual communion when I pray the Liturgy of the Hours, the Rosary, or make a visit to a church or chapel—asking Jesus for the grace to hunger more and more for him and to realign myself to the eucharistic pattern of his life.

Jesus once revealed in a vision to the great mystic Saint Catherine of Siena that he placed her communions in a golden chalice and her spiritual communions in a silver chalice. He showed her this to emphasize how valuable even a spiritual communion can be.

Whether or not we can attend daily Mass, making regular spiritual communions is a simple practice that will bring similar pleasure to Jesus, fill us with grace, help us to live a more profoundly eucharistic life, and spur us toward the holiness that the Plan of Life is designed to foster.

CHAPTER 14

Marian Devotions

Love Your Mother

The *Angelus* and the *Regina Caeli*: Live Your Day with Mary

One of the most beautiful practices of piety that helps us maintain awareness of God's presence in the nitty-gritty of daily existence is the *Angelus*, an 800-year-old prayer that focuses our attention on Jesus' Incarnation and on how we're called to respond like Mary to God's intervention in our world and life.

Recited three times a day, the *Angelus*, Pope Francis tells us, "punctuates the rhythm of our daily activities: in the morning, at midday, and at sunset. . . . It reminds us of the luminous event that transformed history: the Incarnation, the moment when the Son of God became man in Jesus of Nazareth."

The *Angelus* helps us to learn from Mary how to grasp the startling news that God is with us here and now. The prayer helps us to live our lives according to God's word and will, and to act with urgency as we spend our day seeking to love God and others.

The history of the *Angelus* began with three Hail Marys that monks would pray first at night, then in the morning, and finally in the midst of their work. They started to add short, introductory biblical phrases to those Hail Marys.

The first verse is Saint Luke's description, "The Angel [in Latin, *angelus*, from which the prayer derives its name] of the Lord declared to Mary. . . . And she conceived by the Holy Spirit." The second verse is Mary's reply, "Behold the handmaid of the Lord. . . . Let it be done to me according to your word." The third verse is what Saint John describes happened immediately in her womb after Mary's reply, "The Word became flesh and dwelled among us." That Word is the "blessed fruit of [Mary's] womb" on whom we focus every Hail Mary.

After asking Mary to intercede for us that we may become worthy of God's promises, we finish the prayer asking that, like her, we might become filled with grace and respond to Jesus' presence and promises. We say, "Pour forth, we beseech you, O Lord, your grace into our hearts, that, we, to whom the Incarnation of Christ, your Son, was made known by the message of an angel, may by his Passion and Cross be brought to the glory of his Resurrection."

The tradition of the Church has been to pray this prayer at dawn, midday, and night. In the Plan of Life, the *Angelus* is a great way to start, finish, and live the heart of each day by pondering God's tangible presence with us and Mary's fully Christian response. Pope Francis said, "Every time we pray the *Angelus*, we recall the event that changed the history of mankind forever." The *Angelus* reminds us that God has entered our time, wants each day to save and sanctify us, and desires to use us as his servants to help him save others. With the help of Mary's intercession, the *Angelus*, perhaps better than any other spiritual practice, helps us to remember these realities.

During the Easter season, the *Angelus* is replaced with the *Regina Caeli* or "Queen of Heaven." The prayer is from the twelfth century and helps us go from the joy of the Incarnation to the even greater joy of the Resurrection. In the *Angelus* we seek to enter into Mary's joy at the coming of God into the world and into our lives, and in the *Regina Caeli* we desire to enter into Mary's joy at her Son's eternal triumph over sin and death.

The prayer begins, "Queen of Heaven, Rejoice! Alleluia!" Then we continue, "For he whom you merited to bear, alleluia!, has risen as he said, alleluia!" The *Regina Caeli* explicitly ties Jesus' Incarnation to his Resurrection. As the prayer continues, we beg that Mary will help us enter with her into the fullness of the joy of Jesus' risen life. We ask her, "Pray for us to God, alleluia!," remind her once more to "Rejoice and be glad. . . . For the Lord has truly risen!," and then finish by praying, "O God, who through the Resurrection of your Son, our Lord Jesus Christ, deigned to give joy to the world, grant, we beseech you, that through the intercession of the Virgin Mary, his Mother, we may seize the joys of eternal life, through the same Christ our Lord. Amen!"

The "joys of eternal life" that we ask Mary's help to obtain are not meant to be exclusively future and celestial, but something we're both able and supposed to have a foretaste of here on earth. As Saint Paul reminds us, Jesus' Resurrection leads us to "walk in newness of life" (Rom 6:1–4). Once we grasp that Jesus, the Incarnate Word, is with us in our day-to-day life and risen from the dead, it's hard for us not to feel the joy experienced by Mary, by Mary Magdalene, by the disciples on the road to Emmaus, and by the Apostles in the Upper Room.

Praying the *Regina Caeli* during the Easter season has helped me to deal with the various daily difficulties that come from the perspective of the Resurrection. If I'm stuck in a traffic jam, late for an appointment, or have a bad cold, I generally try to ask, "How would I respond to this if today were the day Jesus rose from the dead?" Merely relating the experience to Jesus' Resurrection invariably changes my mood and eclipses the difficulty with the realization that Jesus has in fact risen from the dead, is with me, and is involved.

The prayer of the *Regina Caeli* assists us to remember each day of the Easter season, "This is the day the Lord has made; let us rejoice and be glad in it!" (Ps 118:24). Consider incorporating the *Angelus* along with the *Regina Caeli* during the Easter season into your Plan of Life, so that, through Mary's intercession, you might seize and experience, even now, something of the joys of eternal life!

Memorare: In Case of Emergency, Call Your Mother

At the Wedding of Cana, Mary told Jesus that the wine was running out (see Jn 2:3). Mary, the Mother of God and our Mother, observed what was happening and asked Jesus to intervene. And he did. Since that time, Christians have been running to Mary with their needs, asking her to intercede for us with her Son.

So far, we have examined one way we can run to Mary with all of our needs, the greatest of all Marian devotions: the Rosary. We have looked at the *Angelus* and the *Regina Caeli*. Now we turn to one of the simplest Marian prayers.

The prayer is known by its first word in Latin, *Memorare* (for "remember"), and it helps us to focus with great filial trust on Mary's loving intercession:

Remember, O most gracious Virgin Mary, that never was it known that anyone who fled to your protection, implored your help, or sought your intercession, was left unaided. Inspired by this confidence, I fly to you, O Virgin of virgins, my Mother. To you do I come, before you I stand, sinful and sorrowful. O Mother of the Word Incarnate, despise not my petitions, but in your mercy hear and answer me!

The prayer goes back, in a much more extended form, to the fifteenth century. In the sixteenth century, Saint Francis de Sales repeatedly prayed a simplified form of the *Memorare* during a severe spiritual crisis in his youth. But it was a prison chaplain, Father Claude Bernard, who universalized the prayer in the seventeenth century. He had been near death as a young man when, after he recited a prayer he had learned from his father, he was healed. In gratitude, he prayed the *Memorare* for the prisoners he worked with and taught the prayer to them. He began to see dramatic conversions. Eventually he printed an astonishing 200,000 copies of the prayer in various languages and started to distribute it. It quickly spread around the world and became so popular that Pope Pius IX attached a special indulgence to it.

The *Memorare* is my preferred prayer whenever a need comes up for which people ask me to pray with urgency. When I get the news, for example, that someone has just been in a car accident, or is going in for emergency surgery, or is about to die, it's the prayer to which I turn. I recite the *Memorare* immediately whenever anyone asks me to pray for a loved one in need. I pray it whenever I have a pastoral need that seems unsolvable by human means. I have also prayed it on those (thankfully infrequent) occasions when I've been pulled over for driving too fast, asking Mary to fill the state trooper's heart with mercy. And she's never left me unaided!

Praying the *Memorare* in union with others is a powerful way to ask the Lord's intercession through Mary. I belong to an association of priests that has the tradition of praying an extra *Memorare* each day for the member most in need of prayers. I love being a part of that spiritual solidarity, and I am sure that on some days I've been the recipient of grace because of my brother priests' prayers. The leader of Relevant Radio, Father Rocky Hoffman, started a "*Memorare* Meter" for an end to abortion in America. Several million have prayed *Memorares* because of this initiative.

Steve Minnis, the president of Benedictine College in Atchison, Kansas, started a *Memorare* Army. Students, faculty, alumni, and others commit to pray when important needs arise. Joseph Naumann, the archbishop of Kansas City, Kansas, wrote that once he was heading to Benedictine College to bless its new Marian grotto, but the forecast was for uninterrupted downpours. As he was driving to the campus through pounding rain, the archbishop called President Minnis to ask him to get the *Memorare* Army praying for good weather. The troops rallied and there was sunshine for the dedication. Afterward, an air traffic controller said that the severe storm had steadily progressed across Kansas, only to stall inexplicably outside of Atchison for five hours.

We owe this modern repopularization of the *Memorare* to Saint Teresa of Calcutta, who said it constantly. She also used it to pray what she termed an "express novena" with her sisters. They would pray this novena whenever a huge need came up. Instead of nine days of prayer—the traditional novena, which would take too long—Mother Teresa and her sisters would devoutly pray ten consecutive *Memorares* on the spot, the first nine for the novena, and the tenth to thank Our Lady confidently for having successfully interceded for the favor to be received. I've been with the Missionaries of Charity as they've successfully prayed express novenas for storms to cease so that kids could come to a summer program, for donors to arrive with food when more people than expected showed up hungry, and for permission to be granted when unheard of exceptions were requested.

Memorares work.

When we run in recourse to Mary, like children to our loving Mother, we do so with the trust that she never ceases to hear and answer us, taking our petition with a strong maternal recommendation to the Word Incarnate. Such filial confidence is a fitting part of a Catholic's Plan of Life.

Saturday Devotions: Celebrate Mary's Day

The Christian week has a holy rhythm that we should strive to live out in our Plan of Life. The most important day of the week is obviously Sunday, the day we call the Lord's Day, because it is dedicated above all to God. Jesus rose from the dead on Sunday, and so on this day we celebrate his Resurrection with joy and recalibrate ourselves to seek the things above. On Thursdays, the day on which Jesus gave us his Body and Blood, it is good to do something to give it a particularly eucharistic character (like eucharistic adoration, or going to daily Mass). On Fridays, the day on which Jesus died for us, we are called to live a "little Lent" by doing some sort of penance and by remembering Jesus' passion.

But from the earliest centuries of the Church, the most important day after Sunday has traditionally been Saturday, consecrated in a particular way to developing our relationship with the Blessed Mother. Saturday developed this Marian character because it is the day before Sunday. Since Sunday is the day of the Lord, and Mary gave Jesus to the world according to his humanity, many consider Saturday Mary's day. Saturday is also the day when most of the disciples were dejected because Jesus was in the tomb, but Mary lived that day with ardent faith, awaiting her Son's Resurrection in fulfillment of his promises. Finally, Saturday is the day God rested, when he looked upon all he had created and pronounced it very good. Mary is the person whose *fiat* led to the fulfillment of God's plan for the re-creation of the world. Mary incarnates how the human person is essentially "very good"—and can be so morally.

The early Church trained new Christians to celebrate Saturdays with particular Marian devotion. After the legalization of Christianity, on the first Saturday after the Easter Vigil, the pope would lead the hundreds of newly baptized Christians on pilgrimage from his cathedral in the Lateran to the Esquiline Hill, dedicated since 354 to the veneration of Our Lady and where the Church of Saint Mary Major now stands.

Over the course of centuries, this show of Marian piety on Saturday grew. In the eighth century, the Benedictine monk Alcuin wrote two votive Masses in honor of Mary. The Marian Masses were said on Saturday and immediately became popular among clergy and faithful alike.

When, through the work of Dominican friars, the recitation of the Rosary spread, Saturday became a day dedicated to pondering the Joyful Mysteries, which feature Mary prominently. Saturday also became a day of Marian pilgrimages, meetings of Marian groups, the occasion for pious practices like meditating on the seven sorrows of Our Lady on seven consecutive Saturdays, and for pondering the then fifteen mysteries of the Rosary on fifteen consecutive Saturdays leading up to the feast of Our Lady of the Rosary.

When Mary appeared in Fatima in 1917, she seemed to give approval to this Saturday Marian tradition, asking the shepherd children to consecrate themselves to her Immaculate Heart and make reparation in a particular way on the first Saturday of five consecutive months.

So, given that throughout history Saturday has been an important day dedicated to our Blessed Mother, how should Christians live the Marian character of Saturday?

Some Christians add a particular hymn to their prayers, like the "Hail, Holy Queen," or they pray one or all the mysteries of the Rosary. Others offer a small mortification in union with Our Lady's sorrows, make a visit to a nearby Marian shrine, or attend Mass on Saturday, giving Mary the joy of leading us to the blessed fruit of her womb.

The Venerable Archbishop Fulton J. Sheen made a promise on the day of his ordination that he would offer a Mass each Saturday through Our Lady's intercession so that she would protect and nourish his priesthood. She did. When Saturdays are lived well, we become more like Mary. And there's no greater way to live a Plan of Life than by imitating our Mother Mary and allowing her to nurture us to become more like her Son.

CHAPTER 15

Penitential Practices

Reorient Your Heart to God

Penance: Live in Constant Conversion

At the beginning of his public ministry, Jesus called us to repent and believe in the Gospel (see Mk 1:15). This word "repent" isn't just the intellectual act of recognizing our sin and resolving to change our life. Repentance also includes acts of penance. This is perhaps one of the least appealing practices in a Plan of Life, but we choose to do it in union with and out of love for Jesus, who suffered so much for our sake.

Among the most common acts of penance, or visible signs of conversion, insisted upon by Scripture and tradition are "above all three forms, fasting, prayer, and almsgiving, which express conversion in relation to oneself, to God, and to others" (*CCC* 1434). These three practices are emphasized during Lent but should not be restricted to that liturgical season. They are meant to be a way of life for Christians.

In Scripture, we see the important role of penance in the life of faith. Because of Jonah's preaching, the Ninevites repented in sackcloth and ashes (see Jon 3:6–10). The whole people of Israel— husbands, wives, children, resident aliens, hired laborers, slaves —similarly repented in sackcloth, ashes, and prayed fervently when the Assyrians were attacking (see Jud 4:11). John the Baptist fasted, lived an ascetic lifestyle, and called others to imitate him. He encouraged people to receive baptism as a sign of their sorrow for sin and their need for forgiveness (see Mk 1:1–8, 2:18).

Repentance, however, isn't principally a bodily act. It's ultimately a thing of the heart that overflows into deeds. The *Catechism of the Catholic Church* teaches us that "Jesus' call to conversion and penance, like that of the prophets before him, does not aim first at outward works, 'sackcloth and ashes,' fasting and mortification, but at the conversion of the heart, interior conversion" (1430). It aims, rather, at "a radical reorientation of our whole life, a return, a conversion to God with all our heart, an end to sin, a turning away from evil, with repugnance toward the evil actions we have committed" (1431).Without this interior change of heart, all penances would be "sterile and false." Whenever this interior change is real, however, it expresses itself "in visible signs, gestures, and works of penance" (1430).

The traditional word for acts of penance is "mortification." In this age of affirmation and the consumerist, quasi-religious pursuit of the maximization of superficial pleasure, mortification is almost a dirty word. "Putting to death"—which is what mortification literally means—seems diametrically opposed to the "life" we're seeking. To mention mortification may conjure images of the Pharisees, Jansenists, and Dan Brown's albino monk. We're tempted to believe that the only thing that could come from the subjugation of any natural impulse would be psychological harm.

Yet Jesus is clear about our need for acts of penance. He stresses that unless we deny ourselves, pick up our cross—one of the strongest symbols of death in the ancient world—and follow him, we cannot be his disciple (see Mk 8:34). Saint Paul said that unless we mortify the life of the flesh, we can't live according to the Holy Spirit (Rom 8:13). Self-denial and mortification are essential aspects, therefore, of the Christian life. To refuse suffering, like Saint Peter did when he tried to reject Christ's impending death, is to think not as God does but as human beings do (see Mt 16:23).

So the question for a Catholic seeking holiness through the spiritual regimen of a Plan of Life is not *whether* but *how* to live the penance and reparation to which our faith calls us.

In the past, many voluntary mortifications helped people to unite with Christ's own prayer of penance and reparation. People wore hairshirts, fasted severely, slept on the floor, or took ice cold showers to crucify the insatiable human desire for comfort. There's nothing wrong with these traditional practices as long as they are kept in balance.

But I think there are more fruitful forms of voluntary mortification that both discipline our appetites and align our heart to Christ's virtue. We can choose to live the heroic minute, show up early for appointments, or persevere in prayer or a good work when we want to quit. We can share our time, knowledge, money, skills, and faith with others, especially those who annoy us. We can do what we don't want to do first and as well as we can, or deprive ourselves of something pleasant to which we have a right, since in sin we chose something to which we had no right.

I've always believed, however, that the most effective mortifications of all are not the ones we choose but the involuntary ones God sends us and that we accept and welcome with faith. For example, we can be patient with people who interrupt, pester, or bore us, and we can also readily forgive those who misunderstand, misjudge, malign, persecute, neglect, or otherwise wound us. We can suffer the crosses we're asked to bear without complaint, bitterness, or self-pity, and we can gladly eat whatever food is served. There are so many opportunities each day for passive mortifications like this. And these penances conform us to Christ who was silent when he was led like a lamb to slaughter (see Is 53:7), who returned no insult (see 1 Pet 2:23), who prayed for his persecutors, did good to those who hated him, and loved his enemies (see Lk 6:27, 35) until the end.

Jesus calls us to follow him—from his prayerful penance in the desert all the way to Golgotha—and in doing so, he shows us the path to holiness. Penance helps us to share more fully in Jesus' victory over sin and death, and it gives us a chance to participate as co-redeemers in Christ's redemption of the world.

Fasting: Hunger for Holiness

Jesus tells us, "Whenever you pray," "Whenever you fast," "Whenever you give alms," do not do it to be noticed but only to grow in greater union with God the Father (Mt 6:2, 5, 16). We have already touched upon prayer and almsgiving. Now we will consider the practice of fasting, often one of the most minimized and underutilized parts of a Catholic Plan of Life.

Some Catholics fast only on the two days a year that it is required: Ash Wednesday and Good Friday. Others go beyond by giving up, for example, chocolate, sweets, or alcoholic beverages throughout Lent. To a large degree, however, fasting in this way is the equivalent of praying for a few minutes a day or giving a few dollars away in alms—they're good actions, but far from the heroism that forms saints. They frankly don't resemble Jesus' fasting in the desert or the fasting of the Ninevites after Jonah's preaching, of Esther and the Jews in Babylon, of Anna in the Temple, of the early Church in Antioch, of Saint Paul and so many of the saints throughout the centuries.

One of the greatest triumphs of the devil has been to convince many people that fasting is an optional part of the Christian life— and that rigorous fasting is a sign of psychological imbalance. The devil, of course, detests fasting. He directed his first temptation of Jesus in the desert against Jesus' fasting, trying to get him to prioritize his material hungers and use his gifts to convert stones into bread. After exorcising a young boy of a demonic possession that the Apostles were unable to expel, Jesus revealed to them that some demons are not expelled except by prayer and fasting (see Mt 17:21). The devil abhors fasting the way criminals loathe armed police.

The evil one grasps why fasting is so important: if we can't control our physical appetites, he can use them to control us. We can only hunger for "every word that comes from the mouth of God" when we're able to prioritize our spiritual hungers over those of our body (Mt 4:4). If we can't say "no" to our stomachs, we'll never be able to say a persevering "yes" to our souls. How else can we follow Jesus, who insists that to be his disciple we have to deny ourselves, pick up our cross each day, and follow him (see Lk 9:23)? Fasting is a crucial starting point to the spiritual self-denial that helps us to save our lives by losing them.

In the Gospel, Jesus makes two clarifications about Christian fasting that are key in order to fast appropriately. First, in allusion to his impending arrest and death, Jesus said that the wedding guests can't fast while the bridegroom is with them, but only when he is taken away (see Mt 9:15). This shows that the fundamental Christian attitude is joyful feasting, not gloomy fasting. Because *Jesus is with us* until the end of time, as Christians we should be distinguished by joy. At the same time, however, *we are not always with Jesus*, because sin separates us from communion with him. We fast in order to reunite our whole existence to him. Second, Jesus said we cannot sew new patches on old cloaks or pour new wine into old wineskins (see Mt 9:17). In other words, our fasting is revolutionarily different from that of the Pharisees or John the Baptist's disciples, which was a fasting of religious discipline and duty as penance for sins. Christian fasting, on the contrary, is rooted in love for the Father and a hunger for that which he hungers.

God desires that we hunger and thirst for holiness (see Mt 5:6). God hungers for us to set the oppressed free, to share our bread with the hungry, to shelter the homeless, to clothe the naked, and to care for our own (see Is 58:6–7). God wants us to desire to care for the poor, needy, and oppressed. He wants us to hunger for justice as someone who has not eaten for days would desire a piece of bread. Our fasting unites our hungers with God's hungers, until every cell of our body joyfully desires what he desires.

When people begin to take God's call to holiness earnestly, they recognize that they need to take fasting more seriously. But they often fast impetuously and unwisely. Fasting does not necessarily mean forgoing food for days or even skipping meals altogether.

While we can and should fast boldly, we should avoid four pitfalls.

The first is to make sure that we're not going to do something that will injure our health, for example if someone is a diabetic or struggling with an eating disorder.

The second is pride, either trying to win others' esteem or inflating ourselves because of our improved self-discipline.

The third is irritability, or fasting so much that our bodily state leaves us uncharitably grumpy or snappy.

The last is fatigue or distraction, such that we cannot do the work that we need to do because we don't have the necessary energy and concentration.

Most people in ordinary circumstances can choose types of fasting that avoid these pitfalls: to drink only water (and coffee if necessary); to give up condiments on food (salt, pepper, sugar, butter, ketchup, salad dressing); and to avoid sweets and snacks between meals. These types of fasts often go unnoticed by others and also give us many opportunities each day to practice holy self-denial. Fasts such as these convince us that we don't live on bread alone and help us to pray with our bodies in a way that will open our souls to grasp every word that comes from the Father's mouth.

"Do not work for the food that perishes," Jesus told us in the Gospel of John, "but for the food that endures for eternal life" (6:27). Bold Christian fasting enables us to work for the food that endures for eternal life as part of a Christian Plan of Life.

CHAPTER 16

Bringing Everything into Harmony

Gain Focus and Grow in Virtue

Organization and Order: Discipleship Requires Discipline

We all have times in our lives when everything is in disorder. Our bedrooms, closets, and desks may look like they are eligible for federal disaster relief. We struggle to keep to a schedule. We're regularly late for appointments if we don't forget them altogether. When we are not living and working in a structured way, however, our talents, ideas, and aspirations often amount to very little.

There's an old monastic adage, "*Serva ordinem et ordo servabit te*," or "Keep order and order will keep you." Once we form a certain healthy order in life and begin to live by it, that habit of order will give us joy and sustain us for the long term.

The success of a Plan of Life depends on living an ordered life and keeping our priorities appropriately prioritized. We cannot be good disciples without self-discipline. To order our life is to put something in its proper place, prioritize properly, and then act on those priorities. To live in an ordered manner requires us to have a good sense of what is most important and to arrange our time and energy in order to obtain those goals.

If you have difficulty ordering your life, then chances are this will affect your spiritual life. One way to live a more ordered life is to set goals, even daily goals, and then follow the steps necessary to reach them. Another way is to set aside a few minutes at the beginning or end of the day to tidy up and clear away our physical and spiritual workspaces. When we organize our time and our space so that we are able to think clearly and work more effectively, this has positive side effects on our spiritual life.

Living an ordered life is not what many prefer these days. We live in an age in which people value spontaneity. Order, even an order a person has freely chosen, is seen as a form of slavery. Many are ruled by their whims, thinking that caprice constitutes freedom. But true freedom is not found in living impulsively, because that enslaves us to our emotions and to that which is fleeting. True freedom is found in the structure of a holy life.

Jesus lived in an ordered way and he calls us to imitate him. He patiently prepared himself in Nazareth and then in the desert for his public ministry. He carefully chose his Apostles and trained them attentively. Jesus prioritized prayer, by leaving the crowds in order to have time together with the Father, and charity, by working miracles of healing one by one. He had a clear sense of time, not allowing himself to be trapped by those seeking his demise, but rather waiting until it was his "hour" (see Jn 2:4; 8:20). When he sent out his disciples, two-by-two, to proclaim the Kingdom, he gave them the instruction, "Greet no one on the road" (Lk 10:4). This wasn't a green light to be rude to wayfarers on the paths of ancient Palestine, but rather a clear warning not to get distracted from their mission.

To live a Christian life is to live an ordered life in imitation of Jesus. At the beginning of time, God ordered all of creation, and we've been made in the image and likeness of God. The more we keep order, the more we will grow in God's image. That's the goal of a Plan of Life.

The Particular Exam: Root Out Bad Habits

A solid Plan of Life includes an inventory of where we are, clarity on where God wants us to be, a good strategy to get from where we are to where we ought to be, and the courage and resolve to follow that path.

As in many areas of life, however, we can't do everything at once. Saint Gregory the Great wrote, "He who would climb to a lofty height must go by steps, not leaps."

A spiritual practice that will help us climb the steps to the lofty height of holiness is the particular exam. Unlike the general exam that we discussed in the first section of this book, the particular exam is *not* an overall review of how we corresponded to God's presence and help throughout the day. Instead, the particular exam focuses on one particular good habit that needs to be developed, or a bad one that needs to be eliminated, and then reviews how we're doing, just on that score, several times a day.

The particular exam is a remedy for the experience of Saint Paul to which all Christians can relate, "I do not do the good I want, but the evil I do not want is what I do" (Rom 7:19). If someone has the nasty habit of gossiping or criticizing others, a

particular exam resolution could be, "I will not say anything nega-
tive about another person to third parties," or better, "I will
regularly speak in praise of people or say nothing at all." When we
wake up and make the Morning Offering, this is also a good time
to ask God for the grace to keep our resolution that day. Then
every few hours, we can stop for a moment to review how we have
been keeping that resolution.

The expectation with an entrenched bad habit is not necessarily that one is going to go from gossiping constantly to never
gossiping at all—if it were only that easy to change our bad habits!
The aim is that over the course of several days, weeks, months, or
sometimes even years, the frequency gradually declines. And with
a particular exam geared toward the acquisition of a good habit,
the goal is to go from doing something infrequently or never at all
to developing the virtue and having it become like second nature.

The great spiritual writers, from Saint Ignatius of Loyola to the
present day, have made several suggestions for an effective particular exam. First, they recommend having only one particular exam
point at a given time, so we can focus on making progress in the
shortest span of time. Second, they advocate thinking big by focusing on a predominant fault or acquiring an important virtue,
rather than focusing on minor issues. Third, they recommend persevering in our particular exam toward the finish line, examining
ourselves several times a day for as long as it takes to acquire or
extirpate the habit. At the end, our behavior in a particular area
may not be perfect—old habits die hard!—but we will be changed
for the better.

It might seem at first that working on one good spiritual resolution at a time in this concerted way is a slow way to make
progress, but the saints have said that once we start building
momentum, various other issues in the spiritual life become easier.

"Whoever is faithful in a very little," Jesus said, "is faithful also in much" (Lk 16:10). The gradual acquisition of self-mastery in one difficult arena overflows into other parts of our life.

When I was in college and began the practice of particular exams, I generally focused on eliminating bad habits: wasting time rather than studying, using inappropriate language, making fun of others, or bragging. Eventually, however, I shifted toward the acquisition of good habits because I found that when I made progress, thanks to God's grace, there were multiple positive side effects.

Many particular exams have helped me over the last couple of decades:

* awareness of God's presence at every moment;
* docile attentiveness and obedience to the Holy Spirit;
* constant cheerfulness because God dwells within me through grace;
* listening twice as much as I speak;
* recognizing and naming others' good qualities;
* seeing God in those I serve;
* greeting others' guardian angels so that I always maintain a supernatural vision toward them;
* seeing each person as a gift sent to me by God;
* starting my prayer with praise and thanksgiving;
* venerating the crosses God gives me each day;
* uniting my work more consciously to Saint Joseph;
* and doing first the thing that needs to be done rather than what I prefer to do.

On some of these points, my friends might joke that I have made little progress, for example, with regard to constant cheerfulness or listening twice as much as I speak. But I can honestly say that compared to where I was, and where I would have been without the particular exams, there is a continent traversed!

Saint Ignatius recommends having a little book and keeping track of our reviews. You may find this useful (although I've never found that type of accounting helpful). But most people do find the practice of examining oneself on one point over the previous few hours, renewing one's resolve, and praying for God's help very beneficial.

The particular exam makes the ascent toward holiness more focused, manageable, and a lot less daunting. I urge you to take up this practice so that, step by step and with God's assistance, you might ascend the lofty heights.

CHAPTER 17

Christian Unity of Life

Give Your Time to God

Work: Unite Your Labor to God

Most of us spend at least twenty-five percent of our week—from the time we're young adults through when we're sixty-five or older—doing some form of work. Cumulatively the only activity to which we will dedicate more time over the course of our life on earth is sleeping.

What's the importance of work in a Plan of Life and in God's plans for our holiness and happiness?

According to the *Catechism of the Catholic Church*, "We pray as we live, because we live as we pray" (2725). If our work is done apart from God, if we work as functional atheists, it's going to be harder for us to unite ourselves to God even in prayer. If our work unites us to God, on the other hand, then it will become a potent means of our sanctification.

Work is very important for our growth as disciples and apostles, but some of us behave as if work were merely a necessary evil. Especially when our work is tedious or monotonous, we can begin to treat work as something we have to endure until we arrive at the magical age when we can golf all day or spend time relaxing at the pool. But the Lord who gives us the vocation to be saints also gives us the vocation to work and to cooperate with him in the perfection of ourselves and of all creation.

Before the Fall, God commanded us to "Be fruitful and multiply, and fill the earth and subdue it; and have dominion" over all living creatures (Gen 1:28). After Original Sin, this three-fold work became arduous: there were pangs in childbirth, work in the fields was toilsome, and humans' dominion over the earth became strenuous and sometimes dangerous. Nevertheless, the vocation to work remains and has become a means of our redemption; by laboring for others we overcome our fallen selfishness.

God gave us this vocation to work so that we might become more like him who worked in creating the world and, as Jesus would later say, "is still working" (Jn 5:17). Work not only produces *something* but it perfects us by bringing out our potential. We see this, for example, in the study that forms our brain, in the physical labor that forms our muscles, in the caring for children and others that forms our heart. Saint Gregory of Nyssa once said that through our work we become in a certain way our own "parents." In other words, work forms our character for better or worse; we "father" or "mother" ourselves well by working hard or poorly by slacking off.

We should never forget that Jesus spent most of his time on earth not preaching but working as a craftsman (*tekton* in Greek, see Mk 6:3). He built houses, made tables and wheels, and produced other needed items. Jesus did not enter the world of human work as a cover until the "real work" would begin. Rather, Jesus worked in order to redeem human work in the process of redeeming the entire human person; as Saint Gregory of Nazianzen once wrote, "For that which [Christ] has not assumed he has not healed; but that which is united to his Godhead is also saved." Jesus always did what was pleasing to the Father, and his quiet, hidden work over the course of two decades was part of that glorification.

So great was Jesus' appreciation for the role of human work in the divine plan that he often used it as an analogy for the kingdom of God. He mentions favorably shepherds, farmers, doctors, sowers, householders, servants, stewards, merchants, laborers, soldiers, cooks, tax collectors, and scholars. Jesus compares the work of evangelization to the manual work of harvesters and fishermen. He calls us as his disciples to be "laborers" in his vineyard (Mt 9:38).

Since work is so important in God's plans for us, how can we work prayerfully so that we might keep God's presence in mind throughout the day?

Here are three suggestions:

    ❦ *First*, we can view our work as an offering to God, seeking to make of it something similar to the pleasing sacrifice of Abel (see Gen 4:4). When we do anything for God, we do it better and it makes us better. I keep a statue of Saint Joseph on my desk to ask him to intercede for me and to help me to offer my work to God as he did.

    ❦ *Second*, we can offer our work for a special intention. I sometimes offer an hour of my work for one of the people for whom I've promised to pray. I begin each hour with a brief prayer for the person and ask God to receive my labor over the course of the following hour for that person. Such a practice also helps me to work with greater concentration and dedication. When we pray like this, our work becomes a "liturgy of the hours," in which our work becomes an hourly prayer.

❖ *Third*, we can bring our work to prayer and our prayer to work. In the Morning Offering, I call to mind the work awaiting me and ask God for the grace to unite all of it to him. At night, I examine my conscience as to how united my work was to God, how well I sought to do it, and how I cared for those people whom I met through my work.

Many of the virtues we learn in prayer—perseverance, humility, doing everything in Jesus' name, seeking God's will and glory—are the same virtues that help us to sanctify our work. And the virtues we learn while working—punctuality, dependability, diligence, doing the best we can on any given day—can all help us to pray better. The phrase *"Ora et labora"* from the *Rule of Saint Benedict* highlights the fact that prayer and work mutually strengthen one another in the Christian life.

Work is not only about earning a paycheck, but also serving and loving God and others. In short, work is about being the light, leaven, and salt of our world. Our desk, sewing machine, keyboard, kitchen, classroom, workbench, operating room, field, or boat becomes an altar on which we can offer ourselves, together with the work we do, to God. This is why sanctifying our work is so important to a Plan of Life

Study and Spiritual Reading: Hunger for God's Truth

Saint Paul's spiritual counsel to the young Saint Timothy is not just for him but for each of us as well: "Attend to the reading"

(1 Tim 4:13, *NABRE*). Spiritual reading and study are essential to our growth in faith.

Jesus tells us that we are to love the Lord our God "with all [our] mind" (Mt 22:37). He beckons us, "Learn from me" (Mt 11:29). He calls us to convert and "become like children" (Mt 18:3), and we know that kids are always hungry to learn, to ask why, to seek answers.

Jesus wants us to be as amazed and astonished at his teaching as were those who heard him in the synagogues, on the mountainsides and plains, and from the pulpit of Peter's boat (see Mk 1:22). Jesus came to set us free and told us that the truth would liberate us (see Jn 8:32). Faithful Catholics should never bury the mind and talents God has given them. These should bear dividends—five for five, two for two—according to the intellectual gifts God has given us (see Mt 25:14–30). In response to what God teaches us, he doesn't want our minds to be like hardened, superficial, or distracted soil, but rather like good soil that is receptive and bears the fruit of the truth (see Mt 13:3–23).

Many of us, unfortunately, have never learned how to study or do spiritual reading without extrinsic motivation, like to pass school exams. As Christians, we're supposed to be intrinsically motivated to learn out of love for God, for the Truth, and for those whom we will help through what we discover.

In a Catholic Plan of Life, directed to the various spiritual practices that help us to grow in faith, holiness, and apostolic effectiveness, it's key to focus on the importance of both serious study and spiritual reading.

To be Jesus' student is our lifetime vocation. Jesus calls us to be his disciples. In fact, the word "disciple" comes from the Greek for "student." In Latin, the word "student" suggests a person who is zealous or hungry to the point of starving to learn.

Study is not meant to be a dry exercise in which we just read for a given period or, worse, a tiresome duty or a boring homework assignment. When we learn the faith, we're supposed to be on fire, the way the most ardent fan of a sports team, or author, or band looks forward to going to a game, reading the next book, or attending a concert.

In today's culture, Christians need to know how to give reasons for the hope within them (see 1 Pet 3:15). We are called to have answers for the many people in our world who actively work against the faith, those who are confused, and those who are genuinely seeking truth. Christians need to know how to carry out the new evangelization: how to propose the real "yes" of the faith to those who may be baptized but have never been captured by the beauty of our faith.

It's an enormous task, and our minds are finite. We're never going to know everything. The Holy Spirit is present to help us as he helped the first apostles (who certainly didn't have PhDs). But it all begins with a hunger to learn and making the time to learn things profoundly and well.

The Holy Spirit—with his gifts of wisdom, knowledge, understanding, prudence, and courage—wants to help us to become zealous disciples of the Master, learning and living off his every word. Our learning can then in turn draw others to discover that same Teacher and join in his joy-filled, life-saving, never-ending learning in the classroom of faith.

Spiritual reading refers to the practice of prayerfully studying or perusing good spiritual literature. The Bible, of course, counts for spiritual reading, but because reading the Bible ought to be a given for Catholics, spiritual reading normally refers to other books. Some examples include the lives of the saints and other important religious figures, books on prayer and the spiritual life, commentaries on Sacred Scripture or the writings of the saints and great spiritual authors, papal encyclicals and exhortations, bishops' pastoral letters, and works of this genre. Spiritual reading is not so much about acquiring information but about formation. It is a particular type of reading done specifically to help us grow as Christians.

When we think about spiritual reading, we can ponder the life-altering impact it had on the lives of some of the greatest saints. Saint Augustine converted when he heard an angel saying, "Take and read," and he picked up the Letter to the Romans and read a passage that spoke to him personally about what God was asking. Saint Ignatius of Loyola, having read numerous lives of the saints, was moved to ask why he couldn't do what Saints Francis and Dominic had done. While still an atheist, Saint Edith Stein pulled an all-nighter reading the biography of Saint Teresa of Ávila and in the morning told her friends, "This is the truth." She was baptized soon afterward.

My own spiritual life began to take wings when I first started to incorporate spiritual reading into my life as a freshman in college. My parents bought me Butler's four-volume *Lives of the Saints* for Christmas, and for the next decade I spent ten to fifteen minutes each night reading about the saint whose feast would be celebrated the next day. Not only did I learn about Church history, theology, and so many other subjects through getting to know the saints, but I also found great inspiration in seeing how God helped them overcome their flaws, grow spiritually, and make a real difference.

Of all the aspects of a Plan of Life, I've always found spiritual reading to be one of the sweetest. To some degree, we become what we read, and so our appetite for spiritual reading is more important to our soul than eating in a healthy way is to our body.

One of the great prophets of the importance of spiritual reading today is Matthew Kelly. In his study of the habits that make for dynamic Catholics, one of the most important he discovered is spiritual reading. Highly engaged Catholics read a good Catholic book about fifteen minutes a day, on average, whereas most Catholics don't read any spiritual texts at all.

One of the challenges Kelly makes to Catholics is to read five pages of a good Catholic book each day. If that were done, he says, in a given year one would read nine average-sized Catholic books annually and 225 books in a twenty-five-year period. Imagine how much richer and different our Catholic life would be if over the next twenty-five years we read over 200 Catholic titles! And that can be done by simply reading five pages a day.

It's not that difficult if we approach this spiritual practice with small steps. You can try turning off the television or powering off your phone in the evening— if only for a half hour or an hour. Start to make time for both study and prayerful reading. "Attend to reading" and it will help you, like Saint Timothy, to grow in faith!

Retreats and Days of Recollection: Going Away with the Lord

To live a Plan of Life effectively, we must be willing to make God and the things of God a priority. For some, it is challenging enough making time for God in daily prayer and for the day-to-day practices of a Plan of Life. This prioritization can be particularly difficult when it comes to taking extended time away with the Lord for him to refresh us.

In the Gospel, after the Apostles returned from many days of preaching, Jesus told them, "Come away to a deserted place all by yourselves and rest a while" (Mk 6:31). He saw that they were obviously tired. He also wanted to review with them all that they had experienced on their journey. So he took them in a boat, apart from the crowds, to spend time alone with them.

In a similar way, on occasion, Jesus wants to draw us away from the daily hustle and bustle, television, and gadget screens, so that we might be with him, review our lives with his grace and light, and be refreshed. It's an opportunity to press the reset button of our life, to strengthen us in our struggles, to thank God for his blessings, to see things more clearly, to go more deeply in prayer, and to renew us in the sense of spiritual prioritization that is essential for making and living a Plan of Life.

Many saints and spiritual writers have taught by word and witness the importance of a monthly "day of recollection" and an annual retreat, two activities through which we "come away" with Jesus for a while.

A day of recollection is a period of at least a few hours of consecutive prayer. But depending upon our circumstances and availability, they can also extend to a full day. It can be any day of the week. Some are able to dedicate one night a month. Others will carve out time on a given Saturday or Sunday. Many priests, whose nights and weekends are the fullest parts of their pastoral schedules, make time on a set afternoon. There are organized days of recollection at retreat centers, in certain parishes, and in shrines, but someone with self-discipline can also fruitfully do one on one's own.

If you are going to do a day of recollection on your own, you could find your own "desert," a place without distractions. Some people find it in the quiet of their home. Others go to a park on a sunny day. Others, if they have access, find an open Church or adoration chapel. The day can start with some good spiritual reading or the prayer of the Rosary. An important part is conversation with the Lord in prayer about the previous month and the upcoming one, to see where one's life is going. If possible, a monthly day of recollection is a great time to make a good Confession.

An annual retreat is a more extended time of prayer, ordinarily with the help of a retreat director offering various meditations or one-on-one guidance. During this time, we give God our full attention so that, in addition to all the fruits of a day of recollection, we may review the previous year and receive God's help and encouragement to make resolutions for the upcoming one.

Traditionally, most retreats last a week, which, depending upon the format, can be five to eight days. For those who would find this too difficult, it's also possible to do a weekend retreat. Retreats normally take place in retreat centers away from daily distractions. Various groups also host weekend retreats in parishes.

The key is to make the time each month for a day of recollection and each year for a retreat. Many people are afraid to spend that much silent time alone with the Lord because they fear they won't know what to do or what the Lord might ask of them. Others say that their lives are too complicated and busy. But most of us find time each month for dinner engagements, favorite television shows, and going to a child's or a grandchild's baseball games or plays. We also often find time for some period of vacation each year.

In most cases, it really is a question, frankly, of prioritizing God, the things of God, and the good of our soul. Even the busiest of us usually have the time, but we often spend it on less important things than God. We may have to arrange a babysitter for our kids or a caregiver for elderly parents, but if we're able to do it for other activities, we can do it for God. It's worth it.

Of course, the devil will try to sabotage our attempts to spend extended time with God. The devil hates retreats and days of recollection because he knows how important they are for our continual conversion and pursuit of holiness. So we should be ready, immediately before retreats and days of recollections, for things to come up that try to tempt us away from taking time apart with Jesus—not to cancel but just to delay it . . . indefinitely. Resist the temptation! These practices are key to setting and sustaining a Plan of Life.

Each month and every year Jesus is waiting in Peter's boat, beckoning us to come away for a while with him in prayer. Those who take him up on this offer never regret it.

CHAPTER 18

Christian Attitudes

Become More Like Jesus

Acts of the Heart: Sow the Seeds of Holiness

In the Gospel, Jesus connects the "tree" of one's heart and the "fruit" of deeds.

> "No good tree," [he said,] "bears bad fruit, nor again does a bad tree bear good fruit; for each tree is known by its own fruit. . . . The good person out of the good treasure of the heart produces good, and the evil person out of evil treasure produces evil; for it is out of the abundance of the heart that the mouth speaks." (Lk 6:43–45)

Jesus' words demonstrate the cause-and-effect relationship between our thoughts, actions, and character. As the well-known aphorism Saint Teresa of Calcutta loved to repeat goes, "We sow a thought and reap an act. We sow an act and reap a habit. We sow a habit and reap a character. We sow a character and reap a destiny."

Within the context of a Catholic Plan of Life, it is therefore important to consider the types of thoughts that we should plant in order to reap good words, deeds, virtues, and a heavenly destiny. Such thoughts of the heart—thoughts that express our deepest desires—are a class of practices in the Plan of Life that are meant to be done continuously, in contrast to those done at discrete daily, weekly, monthly, or yearly intervals.

We will focus on seven of the most important.

The first three acts of the heart are *acts of faith, hope, and love.* These are short prayers in which we turn to God in the midst of the day, place our trust in him, renew our desire to do his will, and express our love. Acts of faith, hope, and love help us to seek the things that are above with a passion for God and others that we see in the saints. Many prayer books contain classic formulations of the acts of faith, hope, and love (see pp. 148–149), but we can also pray in our own words, reiterating to God our faith, hope, and love and asking him to increase these virtues in us.

Those acts all flow easily into the fourth category of thoughts of the heart called *acts of the presence of God*, when we recall that God is with us seeking to help, save, and sanctify us so that we may help others. Everything in life changes when we are aware that God-with-us *is actually with us*, risen from the dead, helping us to live with a characteristically Christian newness of life.

Knowing that Jesus is with us and loving us fills us with joy even when we have bad days. If we have a vivid awareness that God is at our side, it's much harder to succumb to the temptation to sin. The Desert Fathers talked about the pivotal spiritual principle of *anamnesis*, literally "unforgetting," or remembering what God has done. Acts of the presence of God help us to "unforget."

Remembering what God has done for us leads us to the fifth category of thoughts of the heart: *recalling that we are his beloved children.* The Christian life is grounded in the *acts of divine filiation.* To live as a Christian is to live consciously as a beloved son or daughter of God, modeled on Jesus' sonship, and assisted by the Holy Spirit who helps us to cry, "Abba, Father!" Everything changes when we are aware that God loves us.

The last two thoughts of the heart are *acts of thanksgiving* and of *atonement.*

As Christians, we are called to be grateful for all God has given us, but we often imitate the Israelites in the desert, grumbling even over miraculous food from heaven. Real joy comes from counting our blessings, even the ones that take the shape of the cross, and turning with gratitude to God who never ceases to bless us. "Give thanks in all circumstances," Saint Paul tells us, "for this is the will of God in Christ Jesus for you" (1 Thess 5:18). Especially before bed, we should thank God for the gift and gifts of the day.

Even though God never ceases to bless us, many times we do not correspond to his graces. That's why acts of atonement are also necessary, acts in which we express our sorrow and do reparation for our sins and the sins of the world. When we hear of crimes and atrocities—daily staples in the news—our first response ought to be to turn to God, to say, "Sorry, Lord!" for the sins of his children against each other and against him, and to beg his mercy. To be a Christian is to ask forgiveness for our own sins regularly (see Mt 6:12–15) and to seek to atone for them (see Col 1:24).

The more we sow in our heart these seven acts of faith, hope, love, awareness of God's presence, divine filiation, thanksgiving, and atonement, the more we will reap words, actions, habits, and character that are genuinely Christian. These simple acts of the heart set us on the path toward holiness, happiness, and heaven to which the Plan of Life directs us.

Aspirations: Short Prayers of Love and Trust

A spiritual practice that reinforces and simplifies interior acts is what the saints have called "aspirations."

Aspirations are very brief prayers—simple, easily-memorized phrases from Sacred Scripture or the lives of the saints—that concretize these acts of mind and will and help us put into practice Saint Paul's command to "pray without ceasing" (1 Thess 5:17).

The term "aspiration" means both "breathing" as well as "hoping." In medicine it refers to the action or process of drawing breath, pointing to the fact that prayerful aspirations ought to be as common in the spiritual life as breathing is in physical life. The word "aspiration" can also refer to a hope of achieving something, and these short invocations help us to express our hope in God in every circumstance. They are the ligaments that bind together all the other parts of a Plan of Life!

Perhaps the best way to describe aspirations is to enumerate some of them. I have several favorite ones that I pray quietly or aloud many times throughout the day. I pray:

"Stay with us!" (Luke 24:29), the petition of the disciples at Emmaus, to ask for the Lord's help in my day.

"Come, Holy Spirit!" before I begin to pray or when I need inspiration.

"Lord, help me!" (Mt 15:25), whenever I hit a wall in my work.

"The Lord *is with you, you mighty warrior!"* (Jgs 6:12), what the angel said to Gideon before he led the 300 soldiers of Manasseh against the 135,000 of Midian, whenever I begin to think I don't have what it takes to accomplish what the Lord is asking.

"Lord, he whom you love is ill" (Jn 11:3), the expression of Martha and Mary to Jesus about their brother, Lazarus, when I hear of someone sick in need of prayers.

"Son of David, have mercy!" (Mk 10:48), the cry of the blind man in the Gospel, when I hear of some type of suffering caused by evil and sin.

"Increase our faith!" (Lk 17:5), the cry of the Apostles in the storm-tossed boat, when I catch myself looking at things with too worldly a perspective.

"Let me see!" (Mk 10:51), the ardent cry of Bartimaeus, when I can't grasp the wisdom of something God is doing or permitting.

"Fiat!" (Let it be with me according to your word!) (Lk 1:38), from Mary's words at the Annunciation, or *"Fiat voluntas tua!"* (Your will be done!) (Mt 6:10), whenever I have to accept an outcome that is not the one for which I had hoped.

"Abba, Father!" (Mk 14:36; Rom 8:15), to recall that I am a son of God throughout the day.

"All glory and honor is yours!" from the doxology at the end of the Eucharistic Prayer, or *"Deo omnis gloria!"* (All glory to God!), when people compliment me for something the Lord made happen.

"Deo gratias!" (Thank you, Lord!) whenever things go well.

"Sorry, Lord!" for the many times that I fail to respond adequately to the Lord and his assistance.

The saints and the Church, in various approved books of prayer, have suggested other aspirations as well:

"My Lord and my God!" (Jn 20:28), echoing Saint Thomas the Apostle's words, when genuflecting to the tabernacle or at the elevations in the Mass.

"Lord, save us! We are perishing!" (Mt 8:25), the words of the Apostles on the stormy sea, in any predicament.

"Blessed be God!" in gratitude for anything or in reparation for blasphemy.

"Lord Jesus Christ, Son of God, have mercy on me, a sinner!" as a simple act of contrition.

"O Jesus, meek and humble of heart, make my heart like unto thine!" as a prayer for charity.

"Ave, O Crux, spes unica!" (Hail, O Cross, our only hope!), whenever we are struggling to sanctify a hardship.

"O Mary, conceived without sin, pray for us who have recourse to thee!" to invoke Mary in any circumstance.

Aspirations can also be prayed in dialogue.

Saint John Paul II used to love to say, *"Laudetur Iesus Christus!"* (Praised be Jesus Christ!) to which the faithful would reply, *"Nunc et in aeternum!"* or simply *"In aeternum!"* which essentially means "Now and forever!" When Cardinal Timothy Dolan was my rector at the North American College in Rome, he used to say the same prayer with us in Italian, *"Sia lodato Gesù Cristo!"* to which we would readily reply, *"Sempre sia lodato!"*

In seminary, at meal blessings and on other occasions, a leader would say, *"Vergine Immacolata!"* (Immaculate Virgin!) and everyone would respond, *"Aiutateci!"* (Help us!).

Perhaps the most famous dialogue aspiration takes place during the Easter season. In many Christian cultures, it's still prayed in Greek: *"Christos anesti!"* (Christ has risen!), to which everyone replies, *"Alithos anesti!"* (He has truly risen!).

Other liturgical seasons also have similar aspirations.

In Advent, we can pray, *"Come, Lord Jesus!"* or *"O come, O come, Emmanuel!"*

At Christmas, we can say, *"Venite Adoremus!"* (O come, let us adore him!).

And during Lent the most common aspiration is, *"We adore you, O Christ, and we praise you!"* to which others reply, *"Because by your Holy Cross, you have redeemed the world!"*

In the spiritual life, aspirations create an ambience of prayer and enable a more continuous openness to God's presence and ongoing conversation with him. They can be likened to the short routine phrases—"I love you!" or "Sorry, honey!" or "Please help me!"—that spouses or family members exchange. When said sincerely, they can sometimes be worth as much as lengthy heart-to-heart prayer.

Aspirations help us to live the goal of the Plan of Life: union with God. By incorporating continuous prayer into our life through aspirations, we truly can begin to live always in the presence of God.

Christian Joy: Know Christ, Find Happiness

The fruit of living a Plan of Life, as well as a specific component of any Christian game plan toward holiness, is joy or cheerfulness.

Christian joy is, first, a gift that comes with living a Plan of Life well. A Plan of Life facilitates a continual encounter with God through prayer, the sacraments, and charity. From the time of the heroic moment and the Morning Offering at the beginning of the day to our general exam at day's end, we are called to maintain a vivid awareness of God's presence accompanying us, loving us, and strengthening us. When we keep God at the center of our life, it's hard not to be joyful.

At the same time, we have to work at being joyful. Joy is a fruit of good habits, or repeated good thoughts and deeds. We will radiate cheerfulness if we regularly ponder the reality that God madly loves us, abides within us, cares for us more than the greatest earthly father, seeks to draw good even out of evil, and always listens to our prayers.

Joy is not the same thing as contentment or a positive disposition. It's the fruit of a union with the God whom we love above every other love. So, whether it's sunny or raining, whether we're experiencing worldly success or struggles, even if we're melancholic by temperament, physically in pain, or psychologically struggling with depression, if we know God loves us and is with us, we can still experience joy. The reason for this is that, as Christians, we know that Jesus has risen from the dead and accompanies us and that, as Saint Paul reminds us, "all things work together for good for those who love God" (Rom 8:28).

If we wallow in self-pity, on the other hand, give in to complaining, nurse our envies, indulge our worries, or live as if we can find lasting happiness in anyone or anything other than God, we will never be satisfied. We may experience ephemeral pleasures, but if we don't center our lives on God, we'll never really be joyful.

A greedy person who wins the lottery, a vain athlete who wins an MVP award, or an ambitious employee who gets a promotion, may celebrate for a while, but such contentment doesn't last. Just like cotton candy doesn't leave us full, so earthly pleasures, even when achieved, don't meet our deepest hungers. God has created us with a desire for happiness, with a desire for joy, that all the pleasures and contentment of the world cannot fulfill. He's made us for himself, and, as Saint Augustine said, we'll be restless until we rest in him. Joy comes only through union with God.

While joy is a gift of God beyond our direct emotional control (see Gal 5:22), it's also a task, the fruit of a general approach to life that consciously focuses on how life is fundamentally good and how our blessings always far outnumber our difficulties. It's in this sense that Saint Paul commanded, "Rejoice always! . . . For this is the will of God in Christ Jesus for you" (1 Thess 5:16–18). It would be absurd if Saint Paul were commanding us to *feel* joyful, because we're never in complete control of our emotions. But he *can* command us to "rejoice always" because the types of behavior that lead to joy—thanking God and others, counting our blessings, looking at the bright side, finding the good in others and in situations, surrounding ourselves with joyful and good people—begin with immersing ourselves in God and are largely within our control.

In his exhortation *The Joy of the Gospel* (*Evangelii Gaudium*), Pope Francis insists that Christian cheerfulness "drinks from the wellspring of [Jesus'] brimming heart." Like Jesus, a Christian ought to emit spiritual sunshine, not dark clouds. We should radiate a zest for life, not suck the life out of a room. Salvation history is meant to be a "great stream of joy," one in which we drink and bathe and invite others to join us.

To grow in joy, we must regularly contemplate and enter into Jesus' joy. Often Christians don't see Jesus as he really is: the most joy-filled person who ever lived. Jesus came into the world "so that my joy may be in you, and that your joy may be complete" (Jn 15:11). But many of us don't picture Jesus smiling. We don't understand that the Kingdom of God is similar to the joy of the sower at harvest time or the joy of the man who finds a hidden treasure. We don't ponder the goodness of creation with Jesus, exulting in the birds of heaven and the lilies of the field. We don't share Jesus' jubilation at the loving hospitality of Martha, Mary, and Lazarus; the conversion of Zacchaeus; the faith of the Canaanite woman and centurion; and the simple receptivity of little children. We don't think enough about the secret of Jesus' joy—his deep awareness of being loved by the Father.

Jesus invites us to follow him more deeply into the joy-filled mystery of divine filiation; we are not orphans but much-loved adopted children of the King of kings.

When Christians glow with the joy of knowing Christ, those in the world who are seeking happiness in all the wrong places will bust down the church doors in order to find the source of joy overflowing from Christian lives. Jesus is the source of all happiness. And an effective Plan of Life will lead us to both Christ and true happiness.

Conclusion

Putting the Plan of Life into Action

Knowing the elements of a Plan of Life is easy. *Living* the Plan of Life as part of a continuous encounter with God is the real challenge.

Just as a baseball player will never become a Major League all-star simply by "knowing" what to do, so a spiritual athlete will not set out on the road to the eternal hall of fame until he or she trains and, with God's help, masters the fundamental aspects of the Christian life.

When you put a Plan of Life into practice, it is good to remember that no one can do everything at once. If you chose to focus on a few practices in the "Time Out" section of this book (p. 63), now is a good time to reevaluate your Plan of Life based on the other practices in the "Beyond the Basics" section (p. 67). Start with a few of the components of the Plan and begin to build. Feel free also to mix and match the different practices, depending on your circumstances and how you believe God is inspiring you.

The key components of a Plan of Life are daily prayer, Mass as often as possible, charity, regular confession, and Marian devotion. But perhaps the easiest and most effective way to build momentum if starting from scratch would be to pray the Morning Offering at the beginning of the day, the *Angelus* or *Regina Caeli* at noon, and the general exam at the end of the day. Together with living Sunday well, that would be a quick way to grow closer to God.

The Plan of Life planning chart in the Appendix I (p. 125) may be helpful as you decide what your focus will be in the coming months. You can also find information and various prayers to aid you in your Plan of Life in the Appendix II (p. 127).

I'd like to give Jesus the last word.

During the Last Supper, Jesus said to his Apostles, "If you know these things, you are blessed if you do them" (Jn 13:17). Jesus was referring to his gesture of washing the Apostles' feet, but his words could also apply to living your Plan of Life. Now that you know these things, you truly will be blessed if you put them into practice.

Acknowledgements

I would like to thank my parents for passing on to my siblings and me as of "first importance" the faith they had received (1 Cor 15:3). I learned several of the practices described here in my "first seminary" in Lowell, Massachusetts, where my parents were co-rectors. It was at home that I learned not just about God, but that he should be loved with all my mind, heart, soul, and strength (see Mt 22:37).

I would also like to thank the priests and lay people of *Opus Dei* whom I got to know during my undergraduate years at Harvard College. They introduced the Plan of Life to me and inspired me to live it. Their insights changed my life. Nearly three decades later, I am still working on living the Plan of Life they set into motion.

My gratitude also goes to all of the catechetical students, parents, and teachers in the parishes I have served who gave me feedback on the various components of a Plan of Life. I would also like to thank the editors and readers of the diocesan newspapers, *The Anchor* and *The Pilot*, where several of the ideas in this book were initially trial-ballooned in a series of columns. Their comments and questions improved this work.

Finally, I would like to thank the many people who have come to see me over the years for spiritual direction, who have shared with me their insights and experiences of trying to live a Plan of Life more fruitfully. The work of priests in the Church is fundamentally to help form saints and saint-makers, and one of the greatest joys of my priesthood has been to work with them and others who "hunger and thirst" for holiness (Mt 5:6).

APPENDIX I

Plan of Life Planning Chart

Some people find that keeping a list of the parts of a Plan of Life and checking them off when completed is helpful in forming solid habits of prayer. You can also make your own planning chart on a computer or notepad and print various copies anytime you decide to reevaluate your Plan of Life.

You may also choose to download a copy of the Saint Josemaría app. The app, named after Saint Josemaría Escrivá, the founder of *Opus Dei*, does all the work for you. You can digitally check each item as you go through each day, and there are automatic links to the various prayers needed to complete each part. You can add or subtract parts of the Plan of Life and track how you're doing throughout the month. The app makes tracking your progress in the Plan of Life easy and straightforward.

If you prefer not to use an app, you may find the following worksheet a helpful template for planning your Plan of Life:

My Plan of Life

After bringing all you have read to prayer, you can use this form to record the new habits you hope to cultivate to grow closer to God over the next week, month, or year. Consider making a copy of the form to carry with you and to review periodically.

From: _____   To: _____

              Date   *Date*

Sunday as the Lord's Day: _____

_____

Confession: _____

Daily Practices

In the morning: _____

_____

During the day: _____

_____

In the evening: _____

_____

Point for particular examination: _____

_____

Devotion to Mary: _____

_____

To be prayerfully reviewed and updated on: _____

Appendix II

Prayers for a Plan of Life

Prayer for the Help of the Holy Spirit

℣. Come, Holy Spirit, fill the hearts of your faithful.

℟. And kindle in them the fire of your love.

℣. Send forth your spirit and they shall be created.

℟. And you shall renew the face of the earth.

Let us pray.

O God, you have instructed the hearts of the faithful by the light of the Holy Spirit; grant us in the same Spirit to be truly wise, and ever to rejoice in his consolation. Through Christ our Lord. Amen.

The Morning Offering

O Jesus, through the Immaculate Heart of Mary, I offer you all my prayers, works, joys, and sufferings of this day, for the intentions of your Sacred Heart, in union with the holy Sacrifice of the

Mass throughout the world, in reparation for my sins, for the intentions of my loved ones, and for the general intention recommended this month by the Holy Father.

Method for a General Exam

1. Choose a quiet space and recollect yourself. Call upon the Holy Spirit to help you to be attentive to the Lord's presence in and around you, and then wait and find comfort in God who is with you.

2. As you reflect on your day, recall those experiences that bring to mind the generosity and goodness of God. Call to mind the reasons you have to be grateful. What are you most thankful for today?

3. Ask for the grace to see yourself as God, who is your Savior, sees you.

4. Review the day and converse with God about the things that happened at work and at home. Think about your interactions with co-workers and family members, etc., and identify significant thoughts, actions, omissions, and desires that speak to you about your relationship with God, with others, and with yourself. Is there something that stands out today? Is there a pattern to this kind of behavior?

5. Speak to the Lord about those aspects and ask for insight to know what these things reveal about you and your relationship with God. Acknowledge those patterns of behavior and attitudes that disrupt your relationship with God and others, and ask the Lord for mercy, giving thanks for his unconditional love for you.

6. Look ahead and decide how you will act tomorrow, taking steps to leave behind those thoughts or actions that diminish your resolve to live as a committed follower of Jesus Christ. Make an act of trust in God and ask for the grace to live your life in his love.

General Exam Shortcut

Lord, I thank you for . . .
Lord, I am sorry for . . .
Lord, help me tomorrow with . . .

Spiritual Communion

My Jesus, I believe that you are present in the Most Holy Sacrament. I love you above all things and I desire to receive you into my soul. Since I cannot at this moment receive you sacramentally, come at least spiritually into my heart. I embrace you as if you were already there and unite myself wholly to you. Never permit me to be separated from you. Amen.

I wish, my Lord, to receive you with the purity, humility, and devotion with which your most holy Mother received you, with the spirit and fervor of all the saints. Amen.

Examination of Conscience
and Structure of Confession

Preparing for the Sacrament of Penance

Ask the Holy Spirit's help to examine your conscience well by prayerfully reviewing your conduct in light of the commandments and the example of Christ. The questions below should assist you in making a thorough review. Tell the priest the specific sins you have committed. Avoid generalizing too much and inform the priest of any relevant circumstances in which your sins were committed. It also helps to tell the priest your state of life: married or single, priest or religious, under religious vows or promises.

We are obliged to confess only mortal sins, since forgiveness for venial sins can be obtained through sacrifices, acts of charity, prayer, and other pious actions. Confession of venial sins, however, provides grace to the penitent to avoid sin and advance in holiness toward heaven.

If you are in doubt about whether a sin is mortal or venial, ask the priest. For a sin to be mortal, three conditions are necessary, "Mortal sin is sin whose object is grave matter and which is also committed with full knowledge and deliberate consent" (*CCC* 1857).

Examination of Conscience

For centuries Catholics have found it profitable to examine their consciences in light of the Ten Commandments. Penitents are encouraged to expand on them in their prayerful review of their conduct.

First Commandment

I am the Lord your God; you shall not have strange gods before me.

❖ Have I really loved God above all things or have I put other things— work, money, drugs, TV, fame, pleasure, other people— ahead of him?

❖ Have I made time for God each day in prayer?

❖ Have I denied my faith in God or endangered it by practices of the occult or through reading or media programs that are opposed to faith and morals?

❖ Am I wholehearted in accepting and following God's teaching or do I pick and choose the convenient parts of his message? Have I tried to learn and understand my faith better?

❖ Have I denied my faith before others? Have I been willing to affirm, defend, and practice my faith in public and not just in private?

❖ Did I despair of or presume God's mercy?

Second Commandment

You shall not take the name of the Lord your God in vain.

❖ Do I love and have reverence for God's name?

❖ Have I offended God by blasphemy, cursing, or treating his name carelessly?

❖ Do I try my best to fulfill the promises and resolutions that I have made toward God, especially those of my Baptism and Confirmation?

❖ Have I shown disrespect for the Blessed Virgin Mary, the saints, the Church, holy things, or holy people?

Third Commandment

Remember the Sabbath day, to keep it holy.

❧ Did I miss Mass on Sunday or a holy day of obligation through my own fault?

❧ Have I fully, consciously, and actively participated in Holy Mass or just gone through the motions?

❧ Have I given my full attention to the word of God or have I given in easily to distractions?

❧ Have I arrived at Mass late due to carelessness? Have I left early without a serious reason?

❧ Have I kept the eucharistic fast before Holy Mass?

❧ Have I received Holy Communion in a state of mortal sin?

❧ Did I do work on Sunday that was not necessary? Have I used Sunday just as part of the "weekend" or as a day for acts of love toward God, my family, and those in need?

Fourth Commandment

Honor your father and your mother.

❧ Did I neglect my duties to my husband, wife, children, parents, or siblings?

❧ Have I failed to be grateful for the sacrifices my parents have made for me?

❧ Have I disrespected my family members, treated them with scant affection, or reacted proudly when corrected by them?

❧ Did I cause tension and fights in my family?

❧ Have I cared for my aged and infirm relatives?

- Have I provided for the Christian education of my children through Catholic school or religious instruction? Do I inspire them by my virtue or scandalize them by my failings?
- When I have disciplined my children, did I do so with charity and prudence?
- Have I encouraged my children to pray about why God created them and whether God may be calling them to the priesthood or religious life?

Fifth Commandment

You shall not kill.

- Did I kill or try to physically harm someone?
- Did I attempt suicide or entertain thoughts of taking my life?
- Did I have an abortion or encourage or help someone else to have one? Have I participated in the practice of abortion through my silence, financial support for persons or organizations that promote it, or voting without a very serious reason for candidates who support it?
- Have I taken part in, or supported, so-called "mercy killing" (euthanasia)?
- Have I abused my children or others in any way?
- Have I mutilated or harmed my body?
- Have I borne hatred or withheld forgiveness?
- Have I been reckless enough to put my own and others' lives in danger?
- Have I neglected my health?

❖ Did I give a bad example through drug abuse, drinking alcohol to excess, fighting, or quarreling?

❖ Have I easily gotten angry or lost my temper?

SIXTH AND NINTH COMMANDMENTS

You shall not commit adultery.

You shall not covet your neighbor's wife.

❖ Have I remembered that my body is a temple of the Holy Spirit?

❖ Did I willfully entertain impure thoughts or desires?

❖ Did I deliberately look at impure TV programs, computer sites, videos, pictures, or movies?

❖ Did I commit impure acts with myself (masturbation) or with others through adultery (sex with a married person), fornication (premarital sex), or homosexual activity?

❖ Have I been faithful to my husband or wife in my heart and in my conduct with others?

❖ Have I sinned through the use of contraception, contraceptive sterilization, or in-vitro fertilization?

❖ Have I touched or kissed another person in a lustful way? Have I treated others, in my deeds or thoughts, as objects?

❖ Have I been an occasion of sin for others by acting or dressing immodestly?

❖ Am I married according to the laws of the Church? Did I advise or encourage anyone to marry outside the Church?

SEVENTH AND TENTH COMMANDMENTS

You shall not steal.

You shall not covet your neighbor's goods.

* Have I been greedy or envious?

* Have I made acquiring material possessions the focus of my life? Am I inordinately attached to the things of this world?

* Did I steal, cheat, help, or encourage others to steal or to keep stolen goods? Did I receive stolen goods? Have I returned or made restitution for things I have stolen?

* Did I damage others' property without acknowledging it and repairing it?

* Have I paid my debts or have I played the system to avoid fulfilling my obligations?

* Have I cheated my company? Have I given a full day's work for a full day's pay?

* Have I paid a fair wage to anyone who works for me? Have I been faithful to my promises and contracts? Have I given or accepted bribes?

* Have I allowed work to get in the way of my obligations to God or to my family?

* Do I generously share my goods with the needy? Am I generous to the work of the Church? Do I participate with my time, talents, and treasure in the apostolic and charitable works of the Church and in the life of my parish community?

Eighth Commandment

You shall not bear false witness against your neighbor.

- Did I lie? Have my lies caused spiritual or material harm to others?
- Have I told lies about anybody (calumny)?
- Have I injured others by revealing true hidden faults (detraction)?
- Did I commit perjury? Have I been guilty of refusing to testify to the innocence of another because of fear or selfishness?
- Have I engaged in uncharitable talk or gossip?
- Have I encouraged the spread of scandal?
- Am I guilty of any type of fraud?
- Did I insult or tease others intending to hurt them?
- Have I falsely flattered others?
- Have I made rash judgments about others?
- Did I fail to keep secret what should be confidential?

For Further Examination

- Did I intentionally refuse to mention some grave sin in my previous confessions?
- Have I fulfilled my obligation to go to confession at least once a year and of going worthily to Holy Communion at least during the Easter season?
- Did I fast on Ash Wednesday and Good Friday?
- Did I abstain from meat on the Fridays of Lent and Ash Wednesday?

Going to Confession

The penitent and the priest begin with the Sign of the Cross, saying:

In the name of the Father and of the Son, and of the Holy Spirit.

The priest urges the penitent to have confidence in God with these or similar words:

May the Lord be in your heart and help you to confess your sins with true sorrow.

The priest may read or say a passage from Sacred Scripture after which the penitent then states:

Forgive me, Father, for I have sinned. It has been (however many days, weeks, months, or years) since my last confession.

The penitent then states his or her sins. For the confession to be valid, the penitent must confess all of the mortal sins he or she is aware of having committed since the last confession, be sorry for them, and have a firm purpose of amendment to try not to commit the same sins in the future.

After this, the priest will generally give some advice to the penitent and impose a penance. Then he will ask the penitent to make an act of contrition. The penitent may do so in his or her own words, or may say one of many memorized acts of contrition like the following.

An Act of Contrition

O my God, I am heartily sorry for having offended you, and I detest all my sins, because of your just punishments, but most of all

because they offend you, my God, who are all-good and deserving
of all my love. I firmly resolve, with the help of your grace, to sin no
more and to avoid the near occasions of sin.

(or any other prayer to express sorrow for sin)

After this, the priest will absolve the penitent.

The penitent makes the Sign of the Cross and answers:

Amen.

The priest will then dismiss the penitent with a short prayer and
encouragement. The penitent should then try to fulfill the penance imposed if it is something that can be done quickly.

The Holy Rosary

JOYFUL MYSTERIES

Usually prayed on Mondays and Saturdays.

1. The Annunciation of the Angel to Mary

The angel Gabriel was sent by God to a town in Galilee called Nazareth, to a virgin engaged to a man whose name was Joseph, of the house of David. The virgin's name was Mary. And he came to her and said, "Greetings, favored one! The Lord is with you." But she was much perplexed by his words and pondered what sort of greeting this might be. . . . Then Mary said, "Here am I, the servant of the Lord; let it be with me according to your word." (Lk 1:26–30, 38)

Grace to ask: To know and embrace God's will in my life.
Invocation: Jesus, humble and obedient, live in me.

2. Mary Visits Her Cousin Elizabeth

When Elizabeth heard Mary's greeting, the child leaped in her womb. And Elizabeth was filled with the Holy Spirit and exclaimed with a loud cry, "Blessed are you among women, and blessed is the fruit of your womb." (Lk 1:39–42)

Grace to ask: To be attentive to the needs of those around me.
Invocation: Jesus, loving even from the womb, live in me.

3. The Birth of Jesus at Bethlehem

In those days a decree went out from Emperor Augustus that all the world should be registered. . . . Joseph also went from the town of Nazareth in Galilee to Judea, to the city of David called

Bethlehem, because he was descended from the house and family of David. He went to be registered with Mary, to whom he was engaged and who was expecting a child. While they were there, the time came for her to deliver her child. And she gave birth to her firstborn son and wrapped him in bands of cloth, and laid him in a manger, because there was no place for them in the inn. (Lk 2:1, 4–7)

Grace to ask: To reverence and love Christ in every baby.
Invocation: Jesus, poor and selfless, live in me.

4. The Presentation of Jesus in the Temple

[T]hey brought him up to Jerusalem to present him to the Lord [in the temple]. . . . Now there was a man in Jerusalem whose name was Simeon; this man was righteous and devout. . . . Guided by the Spirit, Simeon came into the temple; and when the parents brought in the child Jesus, to do for him what was customary under the law, Simeon took him in his arms and praised God, saying,

"Master, now you are dismissing your servant in peace,
    according to your word;
for my eyes have seen your salvation,
    which you have prepared in the presence of all peoples,
a light for revelation to the Gentiles
    and for glory to your people Israel." (Lk 2:22–32)

Grace to ask: To be guided by the Spirit to rejoice always in Christ's presence.
Invocation: Jesus, light of the world and glory of the Father, live in me.

5. The Finding of Jesus in the Temple

And when he was twelve years old, they went up as usual for the festival. When the festival was ended and they started to return, the boy Jesus stayed behind in Jerusalem, but his parents did not know it. . . . After three days they found him in the temple, sitting among the teachers, listening to them and asking them questions. And all who heard him were amazed at his understanding and his answers. (Lk 2:42–47)

Grace to ask: To be about God the Father's business.

Invocation: Jesus, incarnate answer to our deepest questions, live in me.

LUMINOUS MYSTERIES

Usually prayed on Thursdays.

1. John Baptizes Jesus in the Jordan

Then Jesus came from Galilee to John at the Jordan, to be baptized by him. John would have prevented him, saying, "I need to be baptized by you, and do you come to me?" But Jesus answered him, "Let it be so now; for it is proper for us in this way to fulfill all righteousness." Then he consented. And when Jesus had been baptized, just as he came up from the water, suddenly the heavens were opened to him and he saw the Spirit of God descending like a dove and alighting on him. And a voice from heaven said, "This is my Son, the Beloved, with whom I am well pleased." (Mt 3:13–17)

Grace to ask: To live my baptismal promises as a beloved child of the Father.

Invocation: Holy Spirit, come down upon me and live in me.

2. Jesus Reveals His Glory at the Wedding at Cana

On the third day there was a wedding in Cana of Galilee, and the mother of Jesus was there. Jesus and his disciples had also been invited to the wedding. When the wine gave out, the mother of Jesus said to him, "They have no wine." And Jesus said to her, "Woman, what concern is that to you and to me? My hour has not yet come." His mother said to the servants, "Do whatever he tells you." […] When the steward tasted the water that had become wine, and did not know where it came from (though the servants who had drawn the water knew), the steward called the bridegroom and said to him, "Everyone serves the good wine first, and then the inferior wine after the guests have become drunk. But you have kept the good wine until now." (Jn 2:1–5, 9–10)

Grace to ask: To do whatever Jesus and his Mother ask of me.
Invocation: Holy Spirit, renew in divine love my family and all married couples.

3. Jesus Proclaims the Kingdom of God and Calls Us to Conversion

Now after John was arrested, Jesus came to Galilee, proclaiming the good news of God, and saying, "The time is fulfilled, and the kingdom of God has come near; repent, and believe in the good news." (Mk 1:14–15)

Grace to ask: To convert deeply in response to God's loving presence.
Invocation: Holy Spirit, help me to seize, and to assist others to seize, the treasure of God's Kingdom.

4. The Transfiguration of Jesus

Six days later, Jesus took with him Peter and James and John, and led them up a high mountain apart, by themselves. And he was transfigured before them, and his clothes became dazzling white, such as no one on earth could bleach them. […]

Then a cloud overshadowed them, and from the cloud there came a voice, "This is my Son, the Beloved; listen to him!" Suddenly when they looked around, they saw no one with them any more, but only Jesus. (Mk 9:2–3, 7–8)

Grace to ask: To listen to Jesus and to reflect his light.
Invocation: Holy Spirit, build in me a tabernacle for Jesus to remain always.

5. Jesus Gives Us the Eucharist

While they were eating, he took a loaf of bread, and after blessing it he broke it, gave it to them, and said, "Take; this is my body." Then he took a cup, and after giving thanks he gave it to them, and all of them drank from it. He said to them, "This is my blood of the covenant, which is poured out for many. Truly I tell you, I will never again drink of the fruit of the vine until that day when I drink it new in the kingdom of God." (Mk 14:22–25)

Grace to ask: To love and live the Mass as the source and summit of my life.
Invocation: Holy Spirit, help me to imitate Jesus in giving myself unselfishly to and for others.

SORROWFUL MYSTERIES

Usually prayed on Tuesdays and Fridays.

1. Jesus Prays in the Garden of Gethsemane

They went to a place called Gethsemane; and he said to his disciples, "Sit here while I pray." [. . .]

And going a little farther, he threw himself on the ground
and prayed that, if it were possible, the hour might pass from
him. He said, "Abba, Father, for you all things are possible;
remove this cup from me; yet, not what I want, but what you
want." (Mk 14:32, 35–36)

Grace to ask: To console Jesus by remaining vigilant in prayer
with him.

Invocation: Heavenly Father, help me, like Jesus, to do your
will rather than my own.

2. Jesus Is Scourged

So Pilate, wishing to satisfy the crowd, released Barabbas for
them; and after flogging Jesus, he handed him over to be crucified. (Mk 15:15)

Grace to ask: To unite whatever sufferings I have to endure to
Jesus' suffering for the world's redemption.

Invocation: Heavenly Father, have mercy on me for all my
sins against you and others.

3. Jesus Is Crowned with Thorns

They stripped him and put a scarlet robe on him, and after twist-
ing some thorns into a crown, they put it on his head. They put
a reed in his right hand and knelt before him and mocked him,
saying, "Hail, King of the Jews!" They spat on him, and took the
reed and struck him on the head. (Mt 27:28–30)

Grace to ask: To crown Jesus by reigning with him through
loving others as he has loved me.

Invocation: Heavenly Father, help me to make loving
reparation for the ways the world mocks you.

4. Jesus Carries the Cross to Calvary

And carrying the cross by himself, he went out to what is called The Place of the Skull, which in Hebrew is called Golgotha. There they crucified him, and with him two others, one on either side, with Jesus between them. (Jn 19:17–18)

Grace to ask: Each day to pick up my cross and follow Jesus.
Invocation: Heavenly Father, comfort all those who are
    suffering.

5. Jesus Is Crucified

Meanwhile, standing near the cross of Jesus were his mother, and his mother's sister, Mary, the wife of Clopas, and Mary Magdalene. When Jesus saw his mother and the disciple whom he loved standing beside her, he said to his mother, "Woman, here is your son." Then he said to the disciple, "Here is your mother." And from that hour the disciple took her into his own home. (Jn 19:25–27)

Grace to ask: To be crucified to the world with Jesus and to
    entrust my soul into the Father's hands.
Invocation: Heavenly Father, I believe in the Resurrection of
    the body and life everlasting.

GLORIOUS MYSTERIES

Usually prayed on Wednesdays and Sundays.

1. Jesus Rises from the Dead

After the sabbath, as the first day of the week was dawning, Mary Magdalene and the other Mary went to see the tomb. And

suddenly there was a great earthquake; for an angel of the Lord,
descending from heaven, came and rolled back the stone and sat
on it. . . . But the angel said to the women, "Do not be afraid; I
know that you are looking for Jesus who was crucified. He is not
here; for he has been raised, as he said." (Mt 28:1–2, 5–6)

Grace to ask: To walk in newness of life with the Risen Jesus.
Invocation: Risen Lord, open my eyes, as you did for the
disciples of Emmaus, to recognize your presence beside
me.

2. Jesus Ascends into Heaven

When he had said this, as they were watching, he was lifted up,
and a cloud took him out of their sight. While he was going and
they were gazing up toward heaven, suddenly two men in white
robes stood by them. They said, "Men of Galilee, why do you
stand looking up toward heaven? This Jesus, who has been taken
up from you into heaven, will come in the same way as you saw
him go into heaven." (Acts 1:9–11)

Grace to ask: To seek the things that are above, where Christ
is seated at the right hand of the Father.
Invocation: Heavenly Father, hear your Son's prayers for me
and for the world.

3. The Holy Spirit Descends on the Apostles

When the day of Pentecost had come, they were all together in
one place. And suddenly from heaven there came a sound like
the rush of a violent wind, and it filled the entire house where
they were sitting. Divided tongues, as of fire, appeared among
them, and a tongue rested on each of them. All of them were

filled with the Holy Spirit and began to speak in other languages, as the Spirit gave them ability. (Acts 2:1–4)

Grace to ask: To correspond to the gifts of the Holy Spirit.
Invocation: Holy Spirit, enkindle in me the fire of your love!

4. Mary Is Assumed into Heaven

"And if I go and prepare a place for you, I will come again and will take you to myself, so that where I am, there you may be also." (Jn 14:3)

Grace to ask: To grow in a hunger for heaven and in love for
   Mary, Most Holy.
Invocation: Blessed Trinity, hear Mary's prayers for us now
   and for all those who are at the hour of their death.

5. Mary Is Crowned Queen of Heaven and Earth

A great portent appeared in heaven: a woman clothed with the sun, with the moon under her feet, and on her head a crown of twelve stars. (Rev 12:1)

Grace to ask: To reign through serving, following the example
   of Mary, my Queen.
Invocation: Blessed Trinity, bring us one day to share eternal
   joy with you, Mary, and all the saints!

The Angelus

℣.   The Angel of the Lord declared unto Mary,
℟.   and she conceived of the Holy Spirit.
   Hail Mary . . .

℣. "I am the lowly servant of the Lord:
℟. Be it done unto me according to thy word.
  Hail Mary . . .

℣. And the Word was made flesh.
℟. and dwelt among us.
  Hail Mary . . .

℣. Pray for us, holy Mother of God,
℟. That we might be made worthy of the promises of Christ.

Let us pray.

Pour forth, we beseech thee, O Lord, thy grace into our hearts; that, we, to whom the Incarnation of Christ, thy Son, was made known by the message of an angel, may by his Passion and Cross be brought to the glory of his Resurrection. Through the same Christ our Lord. Amen.

The Regina Caeli

(Prayed during the Easter Season instead of the Angelus.)

℣. Queen of heaven, rejoice, alleluia.
℟. For he whom you did merit to bear, alleluia,
℣. Has risen as he said, alleluia.
℟. Pray for us to God, alleluia.

℣. Rejoice and be glad, O Virgin Mary, alleluia,
℟. For the Lord is truly risen, alleluia.

Let us pray.

O God who gave joy to the world through the Resurrection of your Son, our Lord Jesus Christ, grant, we beseech you, that through the intercession of the Virgin Mary, his mother, we may obtain the joys of everlasting life, through the same Christ our Lord. Amen.

Memorare

Remember, O most gracious Virgin Mary, that never was it known that anyone who fled to your protection, implored your help, or sought your intercession was left unaided. Inspired with this confidence, I fly to you, O Virgin of virgins, my Mother. To you I come, before you I stand, sinful and sorrowful. O Mother of the Word Incarnate, despise not my petitions, but in your mercy hear and answer me. Amen.

An Act of Faith

O my God, I firmly believe that you are one God in three divine Persons: Father, Son, and Holy Spirit; I believe that your divine Son became man and died for our sins, and that he will come to judge the living and the dead. I believe these and all the truths which the holy Catholic Church teaches, because you have revealed them, who can neither deceive nor be deceived.

An Act of Hope

O my God, relying on your infinite goodness and promises, I hope to obtain pardon of my sins, the help of your grace, and life everlasting, through the merits of Jesus Christ, my Lord and Redeemer.

An Act of Love

O my God, I love you above all things, with my whole heart and soul, because you are all-good and worthy of all love. I love my neighbor as myself for the love of you. I forgive all who have injured me, and I ask pardon of all whom I have injured.

Act of Divine Filiation

"Abba, Father!"

Act of the Presence of God

My Lord and my God, I firmly believe that you are here, that you see me and hear me. I adore you with profound reverence. I ask your pardon for my sins and the grace to make this time of prayer fruitful. My Immaculate Mother, Saint Joseph, my Guardian Angel, interceded for me.

Adoration and Praise

I adore you, my God, and I love you with all my heart. I thank you for having created me, made me a Christian, and sustained me throughout this day. Forgive me my failings and sins, and accept whatever good I may have done today. Take care of me while I sleep and deliver me from all danger. May your grace be with me always and with all whom I love. Amen.

BOOKS & MEDIA

A mission of the Daughters of St. Paul

As apostles of Jesus Christ, evangelizing today's world:

We are CALLED to holiness
by God's living Word and Eucharist.

We COMMUNICATE the Gospel message
through our lives and through all
available forms of media.

We SERVE the Church
by responding to the hopes and needs
of all people with the Word of God,
in the spirit of St. Paul.

For more information visit our Web site:
www.pauline.org.